1000 practical ideas for home decoration

Publisher: *Paco Asensio*

Author: *Anna Ventura*

Editing: *Susana González*

Art director: *Mireia Casanovas Soley*

Design and layout: *Emma Termes Parera*

Translation: *Harry Paul*

Americanization: *Dawn Bossman and Elizabeth Johnson*

First published in the United States of America in 2001 by UNIVERSE PUBLISHING
A Division of Rizzoli International Publications, Inc.
300 Park Avenue South
New York, NY 10010

0-7893-0666-2

01 02 03 04 05 / 10 9 8 7 6 5 4 3 2 1

1000 practical ideas for home decoration

Universe

Table of Contents

1000 practical ideas for home decoration

Based on ambiences created by reputed artists, interior designers, and decorators from all over the world, and using furniture manufacturer's latest models, this book is a practical compendium of home decoration. Targeting the general public, the book offers a wide range of ideas, tips, suggestions, advice, and solutions for anyone who is interested in decorating a first home or remodelling an old one.

A well-designed interior is not just about the latest trend sin interior design; it also mirrors the personality of the owner, reflecting interests and tastes. It finds nourishment in memories and experiences and should grow and develop, adapting to the passage of time and our ever-changing needs.

1000 practical ideas for home decoration is furnished with rooms that speak of quiet, family-loving individuals; others of practical, dynamic people, lovers of social and urban life; and still others of sensitive, romantic characters who love to daydream. Homes today are not just for show; they are used on a day-to-day basis, so it is vitally important that decoration should be not only practical but also faithful to its owner's expectations and to a personal way of looking at the world. This book is meant to be a model of inspiration for all those who

would like to decorate their house. It provides fresh ideas and decorative resources. *1000 practical ideas for home decoration* presents international trends in interior decorating, from the most traditional to the most innovative, and offers the reader a wide selection of examples that are truly inspiring.

Basic concepts of spatial arrangement and layout, materials, colors, styles, fabrics, furniture, accessories, and lighting have been included, with the intention of covering the rules of decoration and establishing a perfect balance in the interior. However, when decorating the home, it is also important to first look around and compare styles and trends. A house must be faithful to its owner's personality and have something of significance in each room. In this way it is possible to transform a house into a home.

Planning the space's **arrangement** has to be the starting point in the design of any interior. This means not only how the individual pieces of furniture will fit into the space, but how the spaces relate to one another and how one moves within and between these spaces.

Each design **material** has its own particular character, and we can use materials with an eye toward dramatic

contrasts. Natural stone, terracotta, wood, and even wrought iron may be thought of as rustic, but can all be used equally well in a modern interior when properly executed.

The interiors featured in the following pages cover the whole spectrum of **colors**, from simple areas in pure white, through rooms in a limited palette, to those that are an explosion of color in which vivid red is set against electric blue. This book also shows how colors affect mood and how to deal with combinations of color successfully.

A wide range of **styles**, will also be considered. The reader will find modern interiors to be easily understood and rapidly accepted, rustic houses of a timeless, country style, romantic rooms, soft interiors, hard and metallic styles, urban decoration, refreshing Mediterranean environments, and even some examples of *art nouveau*.

Fabrics are practical solutions in decoration. Textiles are often used purely for their texture, but carpets, cushions, and bedspreads are occasionally called upon to provide touches of color in otherwise monochrome rooms.

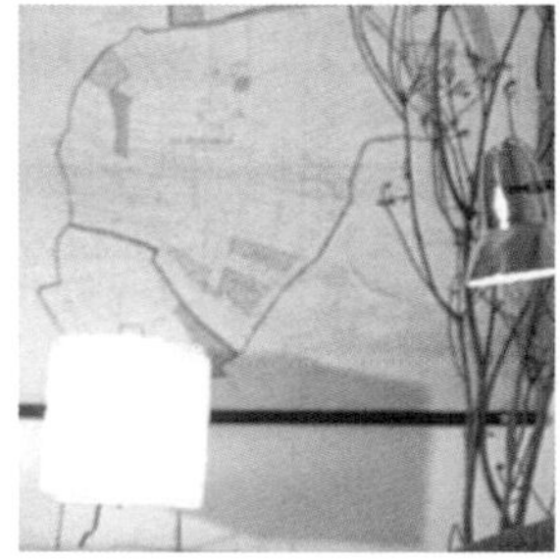

Natural **light** is usually controlled with curtains or blinds, creating an interplay of light and shadow. Artificial light enters the scene either directly into, in the form of spotlights or small, strategically placed lamps to highlight a particular feature, or indirectly, via carefully concealed sources.

Although **accessories** are not always given their due importance, their presence helps to achieve a certain rhythm, to establish an ambience or define the owner's personality. Pictures, plants, small items such as cushions, vases or throws, tend to be used as visual counterpoints or to introduce flashes of color to break up monochrome schemes.

In conclusion, this book is a source of practical, and easy to understand information in the form of an all-inclusive guide for the general public. An explanatory text together with numerous illustrations and drawings help the reader to understand the exciting world of home decoration.

Basic principles of decoration

"The house is a machine we live in."

Le Corbusier

INTRODUCTION

The best moment to decorate

One of the keys to decorating well is choosing the right moment to do it. It is best to decorate when you feel good with yourself but want to improve some aspects of your life and intensify its quality. The main objective of decoration is to create a harmonious, pleasant atmosphere, and we can only do this if we are at peace with ourselves. If we decide to decorate a room in a sad moment in our lives, this gloominess will be reflected in the end result and could even negatively influence our future.

When decorators are commissioned to do a project they have long talks with the client: the more they know them, the better the result will be. When we are doing the decoration ourselves we have to ask ourselves the right questions—it is an error to think otherwise. We must analyze our needs and taste, and the possibilities offered by the space available. Thorough, detailed analysis leads to good results.

Another key factor in good decoration is not to be in a hurry. Decoration must be considered as a long evolutionary process, open to changes as it progresses. We may choose a color or a fabric at the start and then later discover that our first choice was not right. It is never too late to rectify. When choosing colors, remember that a tone can look different on a very large surface; bear this in mind when starting out.

Nor should we be in a rush when buying furnishings or furniture that are to complete the original idea or complement the style we have opted for. Prudent progress pays off in the long run.

It can even be positive to leave the decoration temporarily unfinished because you can come back to it in the future to make small changes or add new details. By making small modifications, we can feel that our home is living, evolving with us as our experiences are reflected in our personality and our decorative ideas. We must be fully aware that the objective of decorating is to create an atmosphere that enables us to live life to the fullest, not getting carried away with passing trends. The best decoration is not the most expensive, or the room that contains the most sought after items, but rather what makes us feel really comfortable in our own home—a true reflection of our personality and tastes.

Choosing a style

Choosing a style for our house is something personal. It may seem that the easiest way of doing this is getting some inspiration from what we have seen on TV or in decoration magazines. However, we should be aware that these pictures reflect somebody else's style and personality, not our own, and if we copy them the result will not be a reflection of who we are. This does not mean that we have to ignore these information sources; rather they must be considered as a starting point and not as fixed rules. When choosing a style we must be conscientious of the space we have to work with, and the possibilities it offers.

The architectural value of the building should be taken into consideration. If the building is architecturally interesting we should highlight this aspect; if it is dull we should push it into the background. When analyzing any project, it is always a good idea to maintain a certain distance, coolly thinking about the space and the elements available before deciding what we keep and what we do away with. Sometimes the starting point may be a particular feature, like some antique furniture inherited from a relative or a stained glass window.

When this is the case it is best to make the decoration of the ambience compatible with the element, or elements, that are going to get noticed. The other objects added to the project will have to match the tone of what is already in place. Once this stage is finished—having been as objective as possible—we can go on to choose a style.

As we have already said, TV, books, and magazines are important sources of inspiration. Other cultures can also provide enriching ideas: we could create a style inspired by oriental, African, or Indian cultures, but never forgetting that there must be something that tells our own story in our home; otherwise we may end up with a museum atmosphere rather than a place we can live in and feel at home with.

The next step is to get samples of elements and materials that we believe can help us to get the style right. The more elements we collect, the better: photos, materials, plants, fabrics, colors, anything that comes to mind. Once we have sufficient resources, we should start sifting through and eliminating those that do not meet our objectives or are not feasible. We will then be left with a set of materials and objects that can be the basis for the different treatments we will give to the spaces to be decorated. Once the information has been collected, we can get down to the project.

We must not forget that there is a very powerful recourse that can help us give a lot of personality to the ambience we are creating: lighting. Lighting is determined by the style chosen. If we want our home to have a period feeling as if we were in the eighteenth or nineteenth century we will go for soft lighting. Of course, modern light switches would look anachronistic in an epoch interior so the choice of plugs and switches is important.

We can avoid anachronisms by choosing plugs that are easily hidden or by installing reproductions or period pieces picked up in antique shops or flea markets. On their own some lamps have a lot of character and become an important piece of the decoration: they alone can create an ambience.

The spaces in our homes must reflect our personalities and tastes. Pictures or books decorate the house and at the same time reflect our hobbies.

A Tiffany art nouveau lamp reminds us of the beginning of the twentieth century, and a green crystal cone shaped lamp shade brings to mind a smoke-filled Edwardian billiard room.

An interior depends not only on the way it is decorated but also on the lighting, a very important element that lends a certain style or air to a space. Special lighting can create a style on its own. For example a row of windows all the same size makes a curious formation and lets in abundant daylight.

Combining natural and artificial lighting can give a space a lot of character. General lighting is necessary and useful, but focused lighting solves concrete necessities and gives the room a warmer feeling.

Redecorating

If we want to redecorate a room the process will be somewhat different from decorating a room from scratch. Redecoration entails preserving the majority of the elements that were already there. The most important steps revolve around the way we distribute these elements in the space and how we improve the decoration with the available techniques. Although it may sound difficult to change a room without introducing new elements, you will be surprised by what you can achieve, even with down to earth (and inexpensive) ideas like sanding down or re-upholstering an old piece of furniture. The result can be a completely new and revitalized look. During all the redecoration process it is important to bear in mind the style we are after; otherwise the effect may become disjointed as different elements added later fail to fit in.

However, we must also consider the possibility of transforming a room, changing the wall color by wallpapering it, putting in a wooden ceiling, renovating the flooring, or laying down a carpet. Just some simple curtains in the windows can give pleasing results. Redecorating is more affordable than decorating but this does not mean that we should abuse the possibilities of what is available. Painting and varnishing are easy to do, but not all wood or plaster should be gone over. A further consideration is that the changes we make should be reversible, because in the future we may wish to restore the furniture as it was before. If a building is old, or unique, we should try to modernize it carefully, respecting the spirit of the original construction.

Venerate what is beautiful. Reforming a staircase may radically change the look of the adjoining rooms. It is one way of redecorating.

A beam across a ceiling could be an important source of inspiration for effective decoration. Due to their solid characteristics, beams should always be decorated austerely.

Restoring an old ceiling can give us an idea of the best style for the rest of the room.

We can restore old furniture or use it as an inspiration for creating rooms focused on it.

Curtains, carpets, and rugs enable us to renovate a room cheaply and easily.

Creating new rooms

Before beginning to decorate a room we must consider two external aspects: the orientation and the views offered. They have a fundamental influence on the room and its decoration.

If a room has great views, the windows will be the most important feature. The orientation—whether the light enters from east or west, in the morning or in the afternoon—determines how the light falls on the objects and spaces, and the mood it creates. We must look at how the colors and materials respond. Whether we are decorating an old room or a whole new house, we are creating a new space, and therefore we must take into account certain factors, and always work (which here means designing) according to a plan to scale that envisages the furniture to be placed and how it relates to the other furnishings. Large samples of the materials and colors to be used must be tried out because it is important to get a good idea of how things will look in both daylight and artificial light.

When testing how the colors and materials respond to the lighting, we must check the material for the flooring horizontally and the wall coverings vertically. Never forget that although plans are two-dimensional, the reality is three-dimensional, so use a perspective drawing with the right colors and materials. This will give us a good simulation of the final result.

Most of the attention in a room with pretty views falls on the windows, so start the decoration with them.

When we have to distribute or create a new space we may need an expert to advise us about the possibilities the building's architecture offers. Often the potential of a room is greatly increased by amplifying it or reducing according to our needs, and a professional is the ideal person to tell us which walls or partitions can be modified and how much it will cost. If we are decorating a whole house we must take on room at a time.

When we are working on a room that has an architecturally compelling feature, keep the other decorative features to a minimum.

Sometimes we will be confronted by tricky rooms, because they are either too maze-like, too big, or just have some strange features. It will help us to make a list of the pros and cons, and what we stand to lose or gain by making the changes. Weigh the decisions before you start to knock down walls or build new ones.

The best solutions for rooms on the small side is to keep the furniture and decoration to a minimum: only what is necessary. Draw up a list of what the space needs and the people who are going to be using it. Homogeneous elements also help to make a modest room appear somewhat bigger.

In small rooms, easily movable or foldable furniture is very accommodating.

However, it is not only small rooms that can set you thinking: large rooms, too, can be problematic. Although we can use colors and wallpaper to give the sensation that the space is fuller, we should avoid the temptation to accumulate objects. One possibility is to create two ambiences in the same room. For example, in a living and dining room we can set aside a space for reading or for studying, or a second living zone, totally differentiated by its style, maybe cozier.

When a room has an irregular shape, with odd corners and angles, the first job is to unify the space. Odd corners can often mean wasted space because nothing fits into them. Made-to-measure furniture gets around this problem and also tidies up the view. Strategically placed curtains can hide an off-centered window.

If there are elements that cannot be done away with, or hidden, like a column, we must analyze the situation and decide if we want to make their presence low key—perhaps painting it the same color as the walls—or making it stand out and converting it into a feature that grabs our attention.

A large room allows us to create secondary ambiences within it, like a study zone or a living area. At the opposite extreme, if space is limited, reduce the functions of the room to the minimum.

To get a clearer concept of how a room is going to work we can classify the elements according to whether they are contents, furniture and furnishings, or the elements that mark the limits of the room: walls, flooring, and ceiling. The coherence and equilibrium of the space we create depends on a connection between these ingredients.

Although the floor normally has the same surface area as the ceiling, it has a greater visual impact and therefore requires more attention. In old buildings the ceiling may seem unnaturally high, an effect that can be neutralized by giving it a finish similar to that of the walls and floor. Dark colors tend to lower ceilings, while light colors, or those clearly differentiated from the walls, make the ceiling seem higher.

Walls occupy a large proportion of the visible surface areas in a room. They can be treated as decorative elements in their own right. We can apply wallpaper, paint, stucco work, or even wood paneling. If we decide not to make them stand out, they can be considered as a background and decorated neutrally. This is a good choice when the furniture is especially interesting or antique.

The furniture is part of the space's contents. To see how the space is going to work separate the elements into contents, the furniture and fittings, and containers, walls, flooring, and ceiling.

When conceiving the new space you must identify zones for circulation and keep them free of furniture or anything that could get in the way.

The furniture is even more important in rooms like the kitchen because it fills up so much of the space. The flooring and wall coverings are determined more by functionality than looks.

Although the walls have a larger surface area, the flooring tends to be more important and should therefore be chosen with great care.

The materials used and the work done on the walls play a key role in giving the room its style.

Simplicity in the floors, ceilings, walls, and furniture will help us to organize the rooms in such a way that they feel uncluttered and radiant.

SPACE

Space distribution

Before approaching the redecoration of an entire home it is important to discover and analyze all the necessities of the people who live there, their ages, daily rituals, and lifestyles. This logical exercise is the first step in ensuring that the decoration is efficient. One of the key questions in any design must be whether it "works" or functions for its purpose, which means improving the quality of our lives.

In the same way we must carry out an objective analysis of each of the rooms that make up the home, balance and moderation are fundamental to ensuring that the space is adequately distributed. Later on we can let our fantasy run free but now, during this planning stage, rationality is called for. Whatever the style we are going to give our home, the project must be approached pragmatically. The views, the orientation, and the natural light must also be taken into account. A plan to scale will help us to objectively evaluate the space available and to try out different possible solutions.

What makes a home more comfortable is not having more rooms or more bathrooms: rather it is intelligently managing the space according to our necessities. A large living room will be a waste of space if we only use it a couple of hours a week. It would be more sensible to dedicate this space to a room we use more frequently, like the kitchen for example. Once we have decided how to manage the space, we can move on to deal with other practical aspects.

The relationship between different rooms

Whether we are decorating just one room or all the house we must not forget that rooms are related to each other; they do not exist in a vacuum and must have a common idea linking them together. Good space management inside the home will make it more comfortable for its inhabitants. If we are renovating a space that has already been used in the past—let's say with uses already assigned to it—we must question why things are the way they are. Habits and lifestyles change, and interior decoration must follow suit. We have to find the right balance between size, function, and intensity with which a room is used.

There are a few basic rules related to the room layout in a home: the dining area will be close to the kitchen; the sleeping area will be near the bathroom and as far away from the circulation zones and noise. There are a variety of ways of creating new rooms or spaces. We must choose what fits in with where we live and how we live. Rearranging internal walls is the most common. Sliding doors or curtains, or even the furniture, can divide off spaces in a permeable way. A sofa and two armchairs will form a living room without internal walls being put up. A carpet on the floor finishes marking off the boundaries between two zones with different uses. Although there are people who prefer long passages, internal walls are now often considered to use up valuable space in interior design and more home owners are beginning to prefer open-plan spaces.

An especially interesting piece of furniture is useful for linking two spaces, or for separating them. One step up, or down, or a half height wall can also carry out this function.

Sometimes when decorating we will be confronted with spaces that are tepid or stark because of the bare walls. Ledges, corbels, or wood shelves will give a little comfortable casualness to the room. Decorating a ceiling with architectural elements like cornices or ceiling roses, which can be added afterwards, also help to give character to a room.

Mirrors are one of decoration's classical recourses. Modern trends in interior design have changed quite substantially in the way they are used: they no longer cover up whole walls or hide away architectural features such as columns. However, they still give us the possibility of making the space feel bigger. Mirrors, usually hung like pictures, reflect the spaciousness of the room.

One way of making odd shapes or features less obvious is to add new elements that create symmetrical patterns. They also help to neaten an untidy ambience. Abundant horizontal lines in an area give a relaxed, youthful, and modern feel to the space. The predomination of vertical lines makes a space seem more classical and austere; they are suitable for a reception room. Curved lines make the inhabitants feel good but must be used sparingly because they can cause feelings of vulnerability.

The rooms of the house

Foyer

The foyer offers visitors their first impression of our home. You never get a second chance to make a first impression so be especially careful about the decoration, avoiding anything too cold or anonymous. In fact, in this room we can pay attention to non-functional aspects, maybe making concessions to aesthetics or including something quite lavish or dramatic to give the visitor a warm welcome.

Old houses tend to have large, solemn halls. The rather imposing, sometimes even dull, aspect of such a room can be livened up by introducing casual decorative elements like a hat stand or coat hooks. However, do not go to the opposite extreme of converting the foyer into a place where all sorts of objects are left about without any criteria. This is not the type of image we want to give.

A warm foyer makes our home feel cozy. A big armoire is a good way of keeping coats, shoes, umbrellas, and bags neat and tidy. However, the foyer is more than a storage space; it is the entrance to the rest of the house and must, therefore, bear a relationship, both in style and color, with all the other rooms. The same principle must be applied to corridors because they too join together different spaces. The house must feel as if all of it were designed as part of a coherent project.

Lighting used to be the poor relation in design, as evidenced by so many dreary corridors. This is no longer the case, so pay close attention to ensure it is up to standard.

No room in the house creates a bigger impression than the foyer, so without going over the top, we should introduce eye-catching elements into the decoration.

The foyer introduces visitors to the home. The style and ambience has to be coherent with the rest of the house.

Introducing a skylight into the ceiling of a corridor or a foyer gives good results both in terms of aesthetics and functionality. However, often the architectural structure does not allow us to do so. What we must avoid at all costs is the corridor being a boring succession of doors, as if it were a hotel. Recesses, projections along the wall, or other architectural elements, can give rhythm to a corridor and break the monotony. When modifications are not possible we can introduce furniture and other decorative objects like vases, mirrors, and pictures. Another good way of breathing some life into the corridor is to differentiate its ceiling from that of the rest of the house, lowering it or making it vaulted. If a corridor is too long but quite wide it can be turned into a library lined by book shelves, especially suitable if there are not any in the rest of the house. If the space has an untidy image caused by having too many doors, they can be disguised by painting them the same color as the walls. Primary doors, which lead into more important rooms, should be distinguished from secondary doors. Before putting in transparent doors, first think about whether what lies behind the door should be kept private.

Besides the doors and walls, the floorings also require attention especially because when doors are open different floorings around the house will be visible at the same time. They must be visually coherent. Place a resistant material in heavily used halls or passages. A rug or mat by the entrance provides some protection against scratching by heels or hard-soled shoes. Finally, think about how the switches and plugs are going to be used before placing them. Bear in mind the dwellers' necessities and the uses the room will have.

S
N

Kitchen

Going back through history, homes were always organized around the fire, or fireplace—the equivalent of the kitchen today. If we analyze how much time is spent in each of the rooms, the clear leader is the kitchen.

Design has never stopped looking for, and inventing, ways of making kitchen accessories easier to use and turning the room itself into a spacious, luminous place, though sometimes decorative aspects have been given precedence over functionality. Before designing a kitchen it is necessary to rigorously analyze how we are going to use it. We have to decide whether it is worth making the kitchen big enough to include in it a table and chairs for daily eating, or if we prefer a smaller room and a separate dining room. Also we must make decisions about the electrical appliances we want to have in the room: the washing machine can be placed in either the kitchen or a special laundry room. An ironing room, drying, or even sewing room can be created. If it is near the kitchen, the housework will be easier.

An efficient kitchen cannot be designed unless it is preceded by intelligent planning. The most important characteristics have to be safety, efficiency, and minimal traffic. When we have assessed how much space we have available we can define the work triangle. This is a concept that divides the kitchen into zones for storage, preparation, and cooking. In fact, this triangle often ends up laid out in the typical U or L shape of today's kitchens. The sides of the triangle should not be shorter than 11 feet nor longer than 21 feet and there should be no door or furniture in the way of moving from one point to another. Place the sink, next to which the food is prepared, close to the cooking area so you don't have to continuously cross the kitchen, sometimes with slippery spillages on the floor, or trays in your hands.Placement of electronic apppliances must also be carefully considered; for example, the fridge must be away from all heat sources.

As modern kitchens use so many electric gadgets and gizmos, and so much specific lighting is necessary, we must plan where to put the (plentiful) switches and plugs. Its important that each work zone has its own lighting source and switch so that the zones can be used independently. Cooking produces smells, some very pleasant, but even so, special attention must be paid to ensure that the fumes are efficiently extracted. Today it is increasingly common for the kitchen to be open to the rest of the house, not hidden away in a separate room, which makes it even more important that the ventilation works well. Smoke extractors are effective though there is nothing as good as direct ventilation through an external window.

A kitchen should not be designed solely according to practical aspects, however essential they may be. A kitchen must have its own atmosphere and style like the rest of the house, and the utensils, gadgets, and furniture can help us achieve this. The work zones should look well organized, everything being neatly tidied away, and ready for preparing the next meal. Apart from their practical uses, a lot of crockery, or utensils, are eye pleasing or interesting in their own right and can be displayed in a low-key way. Food jars, nuts, raisins, herbs, and spices are also attractive and provide a little originality that breaks the rigid formality that tends to predominate in this room.

When planning the kitchen bear in mind that the decoration is composed of more than the wall coverings and the furniture. Other practical features such as jars, pots, and bowls play their part in creating the mood.

Dining room

There are several possible alternatives as to where the dining room can be located. As we have already mentioned, it can be incorporated into the kitchen as an area rather than as a separate room. Alternatively, it can be part of the living room. The third option is for it to have its own room. Our choice will depend on the practical results and our own personal preferences, conditioned by the size and structure of our home. It is ideal to have a space in the kitchen for quick, practical meals and everyday use, and another dining room, in a separate room or as part of the living room, for family meals or when there are guests. Whatever our choice, we have to follow some basic guidelines.

The layout of the table and chairs is heavily influenced by the space available. Avoid, if possible, placing the table against a wall because this would give some people sitting at the table no option but to stare at the wall. Good overall lighting is obtained if the table is near a natural light source and some specific overhead lighting is added, but not in the direct line of vision. An adjustable-height light source is the best option if you want to use the kitchen table for other activities, such as ironing, sewing, or studying. Storage space will be necessary. A sideboard will provide space for all the dishes, cutlery, tablecloths, and napkins used at the table. A dresser or display cabinet is even better because it will provide us with a delightful display that will give life to the dining room. When we are decorating a dining room which is going to that will be used on special occasions for a large number of guests make sure that the table is extendable. The latest design trends shun large tables with a lot of chairs. Now the contemporary solution is a table with two chairs on either side, and perhaps one more at each end. If this is the case, make sure there are sufficient chairs, all of them of a similar height, in the house for special occasions. Sometimes not only extra chairs will be necessary; you will need another little table for hot plates or casserole dishes that do not fit on the table. A little trolley is ideal for this and even works for serving coffee in the living room.

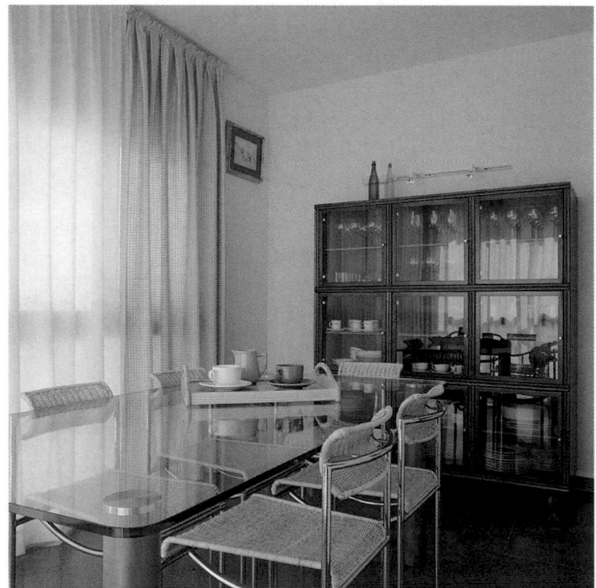

A dining room must have adequate natural and specific lighting, as well as a logical layout of the furniture so that the food can be served easily. However, do not compromise the diners' comfort.

The dining room offers few possibilities with regard to the furniture. There has to be a table and chairs. Although it does not seem to be a space where we can be particularly creative, decorating the table, which is the center of attention, with imagination can give a pleasant feel to meal times on festive occasions. Working with limited resources can give surprising results. If a dining room is visually linked with the living room, the latter will be the center of attention pushing the dining room into a second plane. Both spaces can be decorated with their own style, thus differentiating them. Always go for a more formal style in the living room.

Tables and dining chairs will always be present in a dining room so the style must come from the elegance of the furniture, or something about it which takes visitors by surprise, not how it is arranged. Decorative elements which have nothing to do with eating, such as a staircase, wonderful views through the windows, or a bookcase, may add that touch of character we are looking for.

Living room

The living room is a space where we can simply be, receive guests, or relax comfortably during our free time. The style will depend on the image we want to project. In days gone by luxury indicated the economic prosperity of the owners, but nowadays people are less obsessed with appearances and the priority has shifted to being as comfortable as possible. We are less caught up with wondering whether the room reflects our social status.

The many functions that a living room often houses means it must be much more flexible than a dining room. Careful planning can accommodate all the activities without sacrificing coziness. Design the space starting with the surfaces, volumes, and lines.

The living room can be organized around a focal point like the chimney or a window with views. A carpet and the layout of the sofa and the armchair will help us to define the social space.

The simple elegant lines of a chaise longue, like this one, can be highly decorative, apart from offering us a comfortable place to enjoy the pleasures of reading.

Traditionally, the chimney was the central focal point around which the living room was organized. Nowadays, although chimneys are still used, they have lost a lot of their functionality and have become more of a decorative element, one so engrained that it is difficult to substitute it with other elements. Often a TV takes its place as the object that all the armchairs face. A large window or door can also stand out. When thinking about these questions it is useful to work with a blueprint establishing an axis along which the elements to receive more attention will be placed. The rest of the space is then structured according to this axis, respecting the circulation spaces.

The main zone for social life is formed by the three-seater sofa and the armchair. The diameter of this space must not exceed 13 feet or it loses its intimacy. Avoid people constantly having to walk across this area. If there are two social zones, use size to define which is principal We can set up a little corner for reading, listening to music, or for games. It all depends on our needs. The flooring or a carpet can be used to differentiate the zones, while at the same time the armchairs can be arranged to form a group. Two different floor levels are another possibility for separating spaces with different functions.

Sofas are becoming more important in the living room. Because modern living demands flexibility, it is not a good idea to use bulky heavy sofas, which are less adaptable. Armchairs and pouffes offer a range of possibilities, especially for informal get togethers. Sometimes, however, a living room will be used by just one person and a lot of empty seats could give the impression that something is missing. If this is the case, avoid large sofas. Do not forget the usefulness of auxiliary furniture like coffee tables, magazine racks, or book cases. The best lighting is not general overhead lighting but rather several freestanding or table lamps turned on according to our necessities and activities.

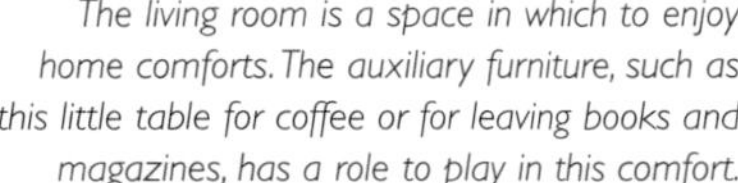

The living room is a space in which to enjoy home comforts. The auxiliary furniture, such as this little table for coffee or for leaving books and magazines, has a role to play in this comfort.

Bedrooms

The fact that the bedroom is the most personal part of the home must be reflected in its ambience and decoration. Bedrooms come in a wide variety of styles, from small rooms with single beds to spacious suites including bathrooms and dressing rooms. The fact that the most important piece in the room is the bed must be noticeable. Avoid the closets pushing the bed into the background because then the room will feel like a changing room and will not allow us to feel at ease.

With so many beds available we must choose the most comfortable and the one we find attractive The mattress is important because our health and state of mind depend on getting a good night's sleep. Beds come in all shapes and sizes so that we can find one that suits our needs and the space available. Working with a plan will help us to balance the room. Do not clutter up the room: the bed must not be too big nor should there be too many closets.

We should manage the space as efficiently as possible because the more it fits in with our needs the more tranquil we will feel in it. Placing built-in closets along the same wall as the entrance door and giving them a common front tends to produce good results. However, if we do not want such a definitive set up, we can opt for using shelves that can be covered by a curtain when necessary.

When you have sufficient space it is a good idea to create a separate dressing room leaving the bed area for sleeping and relaxing. A sink and mirror can be placed in a closet carrying out the functions of a boudoir.

If we prefer a less classic solution we can separate the bedroom off with a screen, a sliding door, or a curtain. In big bedrooms we can create an area for resting with a table and an armchair where we can sew or read. It is even possible to improvise a little office for occasional use. In fact, a child's bedroom should have a study zone, ideally near the window (natural light is difficult to beat in mini-

The bed is the most important piece of furniture in the room and at the same time a decorative element in its own right. The pillows, cushions, and bedspreads play a key role in creating the color scheme and the atmosphere.

When there is enough space we will create secondary zones for working or reading. They will enable more to be gotten out of the room.

mizing eye strain). If the bedroom is only for relaxing and playing, the bed can be by the window to enjoy the morning light for reading. When planning the room, do not forget the need for space so people can move about and open closet doors and drawers.

The color choice is fundamental for a bedroom because it determines whether the space will be relaxing, intimate, stimulating, cozy, or smart. The shades the colors acquire will depend on the lighting, which is made up of three types: general for the whole room, intense specific lighting for the work zone, and soft lighting next to the bed. Make sure the bedside lamp provides light and does not shadow on the book pages when reading. Specific lighting, however, is not limited to the bedside tables. Do not forget to ensure that there is enough light to see into the closet when looking for clothes.

A final point about convenient lighting: it must be controllable from both the door into the room and the bedside.

Take special care with the color theme because it determines whether the room is relaxing, intimate, stimulating, cozy, or lavish.

Children's bedrooms deserve special mention. It is not necessary to change the room completely every three or four years. Adapting it to the developing needs of the child is enough. A baby's bedroom needs a surface where you can wash and dress a baby without any risk of it falling. When taking his first steps, a child will need a space in which he will feel free to explore without getting hurt. When the child starts to read and write, a study area will encourage her to take an interest in things and have fun scribbling or drawing. A blackboard will increase her creative capacity.

Later on he will need a proper study zone to do his homework; ideally it should have natural light. As a teenager she will be free to decorate her room according to her own tastes and personality. Children's bedrooms are usually decorated with lively colors, but choose those which favor relaxation and concentration. Do not patronize the child by filling the wall with cute pictures we think he will like. Young as he may be, he does have an opinion.

A child knows what she likes and will appreciate being treated like an adult in some ways and having a bedroom she identifies with. Remember that the pace of a child's life is different from an adult's. This is why it is especially important children have a space to call their own where they can play and live well away from the stress and concerns of adult life, without getting in their parents' way.

Bedrooms for the young should allow for easy to carry out changes as they grow up. It is important that they feel it is their own private space.

MATEO

Bathroom

The bathroom was traditionally considered a practical space. Gradually modern design movements have introduced the idea that the bathroom is a sanctuary within the home where you get ready to face the world in the morning and wash away its effects at night, taking your time if you are not in a hurry. The aesthetics of the bathroom have become more understated and ingenious. Bathroom hardware, such as the toilet, which used to be neither beautiful nor light-hearted, is now a design object that needn't be hidden. Comfort, feeling good, and a pragmatic approach must take priority over everything else.

A bathroom must feel intimate, a place where you can get away from the rest of the house and from the world—a room to relax in. People today take more showers than baths, so walk-in shower stalls have been designed to be fun and functional. Bathrooms are especially challenging, first because everything is in a fixed spot so you can't rearrange or suddenly redecorate. Second, the technicalities of plumbing require special preparation. Contact a specialist to take measurements and do installations. Put comfort first and make sure there is sufficient room for doing everything, like shaving, drying your hair, and putting on makeup.

Contemporary bathrooms must be as elegant as they are functional.

If space is at a premium we will have to objectively decide what can be included and what has to be left out. For example, do not cram a bidet into a small space. If there is not enough room for a bathtub, install a shower stall. Of course, the have-it-all solution of a main bathroom with a tub and shower plus a toilet room for guests is what we would all like. Moreover, it is great if the children can have their own bathroom, too.

If we are so lucky as to have plenty of space we can install a Jacuzzi or sauna, or even a small place for working out or stretching, provided that this accomodates the family members' real needs and is not a passing fad. Think three-dimensionally because when you have done all the fitting and measuring you do not want unexpected surprises such as not being able to raise your arms in the shower.

The lighting must be considered from the beginning of the planning process because cables are unsightly and even more complicated to install when there are also plumbing feeds in the room. Take care of this question before putting up, or laying down, the tiles or slates on the walls and floor. We can move away from traditional bathroom decoration, that is to say, tiles, by going for warmer decoration like stucco work, limestone, or merbau, a very oily wood. Marble is more stylish than tiles and fits in with cutting edge design, assuming a bold style is what we are after. We may settle on a more traditional bathroom and stick with tiles. However, be careful not to tile right up to the ceiling because it makes the space seem smaller and dreary. The flooring material is decided upon in light of how many people will be using the room, and how often. Parquet gives a softer bathroom but is extremely delicate, especially to water. This leads us to maintenance. Water also stains glass and stainless steel, so bear in mind the time and expense required to keep everything shiny.

Slickly decorated, the bathroom can become an aesthetically relaxing aesthetic room with crisp lines. Using the right colors gives a sensation of cleanliness and hygiene. However, this does not mean that warm materials like wood have to be ruled out. Once adequately treated, they can be totally suitable.A bathroom has to adapt to different seasons: in summer we want to cool off and freshen up, while in winter we want to bathe feeling cozy and snug.

We can also include some features that give the bathroom a personal touch. Framed prints (humidity protected) look good, and plants are especially nice during the summer with the window open.

The materials used in the bathroom are vital because they determine how comfortable it is. Details, accessories and complements will make the room cozy enough for you to feel good there.

Natural daylight is a real winner in a space that requires bright lighting. If this is not possible use halogen lamps for the pure, intense light they offer. The general lighting can be provided by fixtures in the ceiling, but shaving and putting on makeup require specific lighting such as in an actor's dressing room.

Studio or office

The space dedicated to studying or working must be tranquil and relaxing so that you can keep your mind on the job or on what you are reading. One possibility is to create a library, though this is associated more nowadays with old, very formal homes. In more modern houses, books are often placed in hallways, the living room or even the dining room due to the lack of space. This solution is fine but do not count on getting enough peace and quiet when you want to shut yourself away and do work.

The library in its own right presents interesting decorative material. Many people love leafing through books. A well-arranged book shelf, with the different colors of jackets and spines visible can be aesthetically attractive. This easy-to-implement idea should be topped off with framed pictures, prints, posters, or classy ornaments that add just the right amount of originality. Video equipment, CDs, and a collection of tapes also logically fit into a modern library. This is functional decoration because, after all, books are for reading and not just to be admired (though some books are valuable collectors' items). The ambience can be classic if we use traditional wood shelving, or we can be more creative and have metal or glass shelves, much more weightless in appearance and therefore less visible. This will help us get away from the stuffy image of the classic library. If the books are very high up we will need a ladder. A second solution if we are short on shelf space is to have a sliding shelf cabinet on rails: the front shelf is slid back to reveal the second row of books behind it.

The most important thing about an office is that it must be comfortable. As well as the shelves for books and videos, it will need cupboards and drawers for papers and magazines.

Adequate, specific lighting is a must if we are going to work efficiently.

Lofts

In the world of design "loft" is a word that has grown out of its old dictionary definition: "a room or the like within a sloping roof or the upper story of a warehouse, mercantile building, or factory." The concept came from the US, especially in cities like New York, where old industrial buildings were turned into places for living and run-down areas were revitalized.

Turning an industrial building into a residential one offers interesting material for the designer. These spaces are usually open-plan, and even after the conversion normally only the bathroom and sometimes the kitchen are closed off. The rest of the space is dedicated to multifunctional use. Of course, this type of arrangement is not suitable for children and parents—there is not enough privacy—and loft dwellers tend to be single people or couples. Lofts are great for taking advantage of small spaces because walls eat up both light and flexibility. If creatively designed and decorated, a loft can be stunning, but space limitation means thorough planning is required.

The concept of using just one space for everything poses a challenge for loft designers. They have to be innovative to come up with alluring and comfortable interior designs in often relatively small spaces (which also allowed for a multitude of activities). Consequently the furniture choice and arrangement especially relevant.

Warehouses always had high ceilings so lofts are perfect for creating gallery-style bedrooms overlooking the principal space and enjoying a measure of privacy. Below this bedroom perched up near the ceiling, the bathroom and kitchen can be installed thus making these two service rooms independent from the rest of the house.

The staircase leading up to the bedroom is an opportunity to add a touch of personality, but it must fit in with the "loft philosophy," which shuns chunky volumes. The answer is for it to veer toward being transparent, doing away with the traditional walls. The best materials are iron or wood because they allow sculptural elements to be created. However, a particular loft space may not be suitable for a gallery bedroom and then the most efficient solution is to separate off the latter using closets (but not reaching up to the ceiling), or screen partitions. Of course, sometimes no separation of the bedroom is necessary.

Barriers between rooms are certainly being broken down but this is much less the case with bathrooms. Always be on the lookout for ways of integrating the bathtub or shower stall into the space, using it as another decorative feature.

The kitchen can be totally open-plan: it need not be a replica of a traditional kitchen but rather should tend toward all possible forms of integration with the living room and the dining room. In fact, coming up with a kitchen that does not look like one but is as pragmatic as the most orthodox-looking kitchen is a design challenge. In our scale of values, aesthetics have not dislodged functionality.

Necessities will determine how the space is divided, although, generally, the kitchen, the dining room, the living room, and often the bedroom, are all open-plan. Often the bathroom is the only fullly separate room requiring special treatment.

In these permeable living spaces the kitchen can be integrated into the dining room but still retain its independence. An eating area can be set aside in the kitchen using a high table or a counter with stools.

The dining room can double as a work or study desk, its eating function being reserved for defined occasions. The living room tends to be the embodiment of a multifunctional space adaptable to diverse situations. It is a room in which a chimney looks good and works well as the central feature around which everything is structured. Besides, there is no cozier way of keeping warm and snug.

What may have been medium-sized for a factory offers plentiful space for a residence. However, the loft concept is also perfectly valid for small spaces like apartments or studios and is a philosophy that can be carried over into the decoration of multifunctional rooms in typical houses. A case in point is the children's homework room, which can also sometimes be used for relaxing or as a guest room.

The loft philosophy helps us to conceive an open plan multifunctional space in which zones are made independent with the techniques discussed so far in this book. In order to work effectively, these spaces require these techniques to be employed as imaginatively as possible. Wall colors, floorings, and carpets can mark off ambiences and activities. Tall pieces of furniture offer visual discontinuity but have the disadvantages of creating clutter in small spaces rather than blending together in a neat composition. Sliding doors, curtains, and screens should always be considered. They can be withdrawn when the moment so requires. The furniture should also be adaptable to different tasks. Adjustable-height tables, or ones that open up or fold away improve the flexibility. We probably will need bookshelves, armchairs, and sofa beds. Another way of defining zones is to use lighting, while remembering that artificial lighting during the day should only be turned on because of a lack of natural light.

An open-plan space allows us to create bright, uncluttered ambiences, which are easily adaptable to different situations.

LIGHT

Natural lighting

Natural lighting is an important element in bringing out the best in the color scheme. If light enters through side windows, a dark ceiling will make the room look gloomy. If the light comes in obliquely it is advisable to paint the floors a pale color. High buildings or spaces awash with natural light can become too dazzling if the light is reflected off white walls. A medium tone is necessary because a dark wall would contrast too strongly with the luminous window. Bearing in mind all these factors, you should analyze the daylight in your house throughout the day and then plan the artificial lighting.

Artificial light

When we are planning the lighting in a house we must bear in mind certain characteristics of human vision. The human eye is designed to function at light intensities that range from 100,000 lux, the brightness of midday, down to half a lux at midnight. The eye needs a short period of adaptation when moving from strong lighting to a darker area and this is why we must create zones of intermediate light within the house, for example, between the brightness of a wall illuminated by the sunlight from a window to the half-shadow of a hallway. Another factor to consider is monotony and tired vision.

The human eye is used to constant light fluctuations. This does not happen with artificial lighting so we must aim at offering the eye shadowy spaces contrasted by brighter ones. The eye is then always moving about and refocusing. Light shades, diffusers, and the range of light bulbs now available mean that it is possible to avoid glare from bright sources placed against dark backgrounds.

Lighting and decoration are closely related. Their attractiveness is mutually dependent. The general lighting depends on how the light is reflected off the surfaces and how much is absorbed. In turn, the color we perceive the walls and the furniture in a room to be depends on how much light comes in and at what angle. White, obviously, is the best reflector and has to be used on large ceilings because it throws light back down toward the floor giving good general lighting. In a small room, pale colored walls distribute the light to an acceptable standard, which means, if you wish, you can paint the ceiling a darker tone.

Lighting is one ingredient that decoration exploits: do not turn your back on the possibilities. Controlling the lighting of a space creates mood and captures the moment. Some theatrical effects will give an original touch to the style we are seeking.

TUMI
UROS

General lighting

Lighting is not just a question of seeing what you are doing; it has to create the right atmosphere. First, we must deal with the general lighting, also known as the ambient lighting, provided by fixtures in the ceiling or on the wall. Normally they do not give out enough light for specific tasks in defined areas and therefore we complement the general lighting with specific lighting.

General lighting refers to light that is similar throughout the house, making sure we are comfortable walking from one room to another. Lighting is in vogue and the market offers a wide range of lamp designs to fit in with all decoration styles and ambiences. There are uplighters, downlighters, floor lamps, halogen tubes, and spotlights. Specialists will advise us about the most suitable lighting source for each type of activity and space. Adjustable lighting—intensifying or dimming the lighting depending on the moment—opens up even more possibilities. For safety, let an electrician do the wiring while at the same time informing us about new technologies coming into the market and offering new possibilities.

Specific lighting

It almost goes without saying that the first standard to consider when lighting a specific zone is to ensure that you can see what you are doing. The light must fall where it is needed without creating annoying shadows or reflections. For desks and tables the key factor is to avoid the light being blocked out by the writing or drawing arm, so take into account whether the user is left or right-handed. A right-handed person needs the light to come from their left.

For activities such as ironing, light should fall obliquely so that we can see the creases in the clothes. A general rule is that the shadow ought to be at eye level. If it is higher up it blinds us, and, alternatively, if it is too close to the book we are reading it will be annoying. A way around this problem is to have adjustable lamps, suitable for every type of activity.

It is important to balance specific and general lighting because strong contrasts hurt the eyes. A good guideline is for the surrounding area to be at least a third as bright as the work surface. In rooms like the dining room, where the principle pieces of furniture can be moved around, try to find a better solution than the traditional fixed lamp

A small, strategically placed lamp lights up a specific area.

Pay attention to the specific lighting in work and study zones, such as the kitchen, the bathroom and the office. Avoiding eye-strain is vital for comfort and quality of life.

hanging from the ceiling; it is not flexible enough. Aware of this problem, designers have come up with ceiling lamps adjustable according to our needs. Floor lamps are another solution to be considered in the dining room because they offer a cozy ambience impossible to get with downlighters or hanging lamps.

Free-standing lamps and table lamps are especially easy to use because of their mobility.

DO

Use the general lighting to soften the strong contrasts.

Make sure that the specific lighting is sufficient for the task being done.

Cleverly position the hanging lamps so that they neither dazzle nor create annoying reflections.

DO NOT

Leave corridors or small rooms relatively dimly lit in comparison with the rooms that receive daylight directly.

Place light sources in such a way that they create shadows in work areas.

Go without specific lighting because it makes many tasks more comfortable to perform and creates a mood in such a way that general lighting cannot.

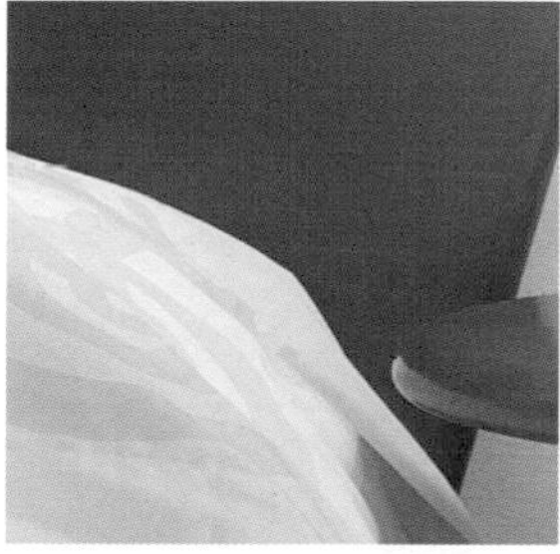

Lamps are some of the most important decorative accessories, not only due to the light they offer but also because they offer the opportunity to highlight certain aspects of the interior design.

Specific lighting is even more important in spaces without natural light because it must create the mood on its own.

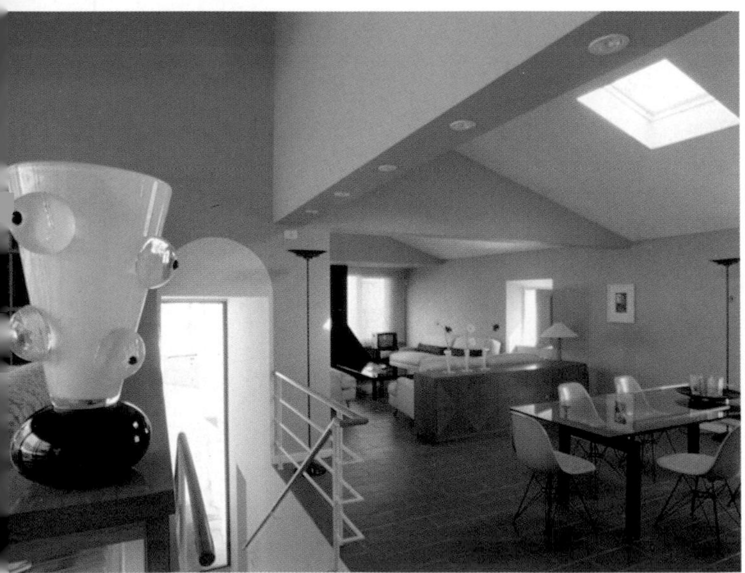

TEN HELPFUL HINTS

1 Control the light using blinds and curtains, always adapting it to the needs of every moment.

2 Soften the contrast produced by a window and the dark surrounding wall by focusing artificial light onto the latter.

3 Emphasize the beauty of an especially compelling piece of furniture by spotlighting it.

4 In work areas the specific lighting must be from the left for right-handed people and vice versa.

5 The direct light from a hanging lamp must always be below eye-level, otherwise it will blind us.

6 Use subtle general lighting so that the transition from a bright area to a darker one is not painful for the eyes

7 Make sure that the light in a work area is compensated by the surrounding lighting so that you do not strain your eyes.

8 Use free-standing lamps and floor lamps in spaces where the furniture is frequently rearranged.These types of lamps offer adaptable solutions.

9 A highly reflective surface (the whiter the better) helps to multiply the light and to diffuse it all over the space.

10 In small rooms pale-colored walls give acceptable lighting.A darker ceiling breaks the monotony and provides contrast.

COLORS

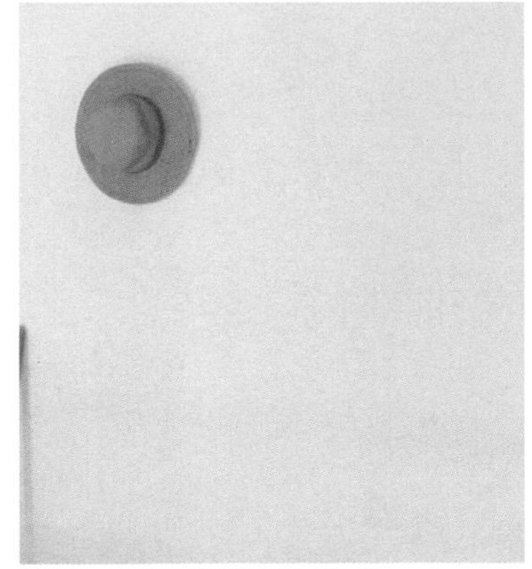

Choosing colors

In ways that sometimes surprise us, color is heavily influential in determining the look of a space. Color affects the way a space looks as well as the way furniture is seen. Color offers an endless range of shades and subtleties found not only in paint: curtains, tablecloths, place mats, bedlinen, carpets, toilet hardware, and other details give us the possibility to experiment with this variable.

The lighting can also enhance the colors of a room. Badly lit colors will give a drab interior design. However, tastefully chosen colored light bulbs, used with lamp shades, usually give a cozy atmosphere. Having a sense of color is probably something you are born with, but if you do not have it, don't despair. There are some tricks that can help you to get the most out of color while playing it safe. Take, for example, some color combinations we have already seen. Abstract pictures such as prints or fashion photos are especially good for this purpose. What matters is that it shows us a color combination we find attractive. Analyze each of the tones; determine which colors, and in what proportions, complement them to give the final result. The next step is to apply the same scheme to the space being decorated. A good color scheme means the interior is coherent. This trick will work just as well for the whole house or just one room.

Color

It is important that the colors in the different rooms around the house come together coherently. However, this does not mean that we have to limit ourselves to the same colors through the whole house. Try to find the color which best suits each room, bearing in mind the connotations and sensations the colors produce. For the spaces where we relax, use tranquilizing colors; for the study, use stimulating colors. It is a somewhat daunting task but we must not be put off. The psychological influence of colors has been proven scientifically, so we should pay attention.

Joining rooms together with color

In modern interior design white has come very much mainstream almost to the exclusion of other colors. This predilection does not always pay off because sometimes white is too cold. However, it is a special color and must always be considered as a possibility.

Color is a simple way of giving a sense of unity to the different rooms the house. The entrance foyer offers the first impression of the house so the color game starts here. As you go on from the foyer, the same colors need not be repeated room after room. Take a walk around the house seeing how the rooms lead into and out of each other, observing the relationship between them.

There are other ways of linking spaces together, like the flooring, the pictures and the lighting. In each room or space we can decide which feature we want to bring to the forefront and then use color to set the right context. Color is clearly the most visible linking factor between separate rooms and is ideal for giving coherence to the decoration scheme of a whole house. If, for example, we wish to strengthen the relationship between the living room and the main bedroom we must first analyze the colors which dominate in each room.

TEN HELPFUL HINTS

The next step is to put in little dashes of the color dominating in one room in the next room. We can use small details like ornaments, flowers, a bed cushion, or lamps. If the theme in the dining room is yellow, some yellow details in the bedroom will link the rooms naturally. It is not always so easy to establish a relationship because colors do not always match. There are other ways to link rooms: by using furniture, flooring or lighting. The importance of linking rooms together by having something in common should not be underestimated, otherwise the final result could be a disjointed house in which each room looks as if it were decorated by a different person.

1 Brighten up the darker spaces by painting the walls in pale colors.

2 If we paint a high ceiling a dark color, it will look lower.

3 A light blue or a gray makes a small room seem wider.

4 Use the wall colors to mark off areas according to activities.

5 Red and reddish tones are bold, exciting colors which stimulate movement. They are especially suitable for work areas.

6 Yellows are warm, bright colors, ideal for dark spaces to make us feel cozy

7 Green is intrinsically linked to life; it reminds us of nature and is perfect for interiors we want to connect with outside.

8 Blues are fresh, harmonious, and easy to combine. They remind us of vast extensions of sea and sky.

9 To make a room more luminous, we can paint the walls in light colors and introduce dashes of color through the furniture, complements, and ornaments.

10 Neutral colors like beiges and browns combine well with other tones and give the room a natural feel.

FURNITURE

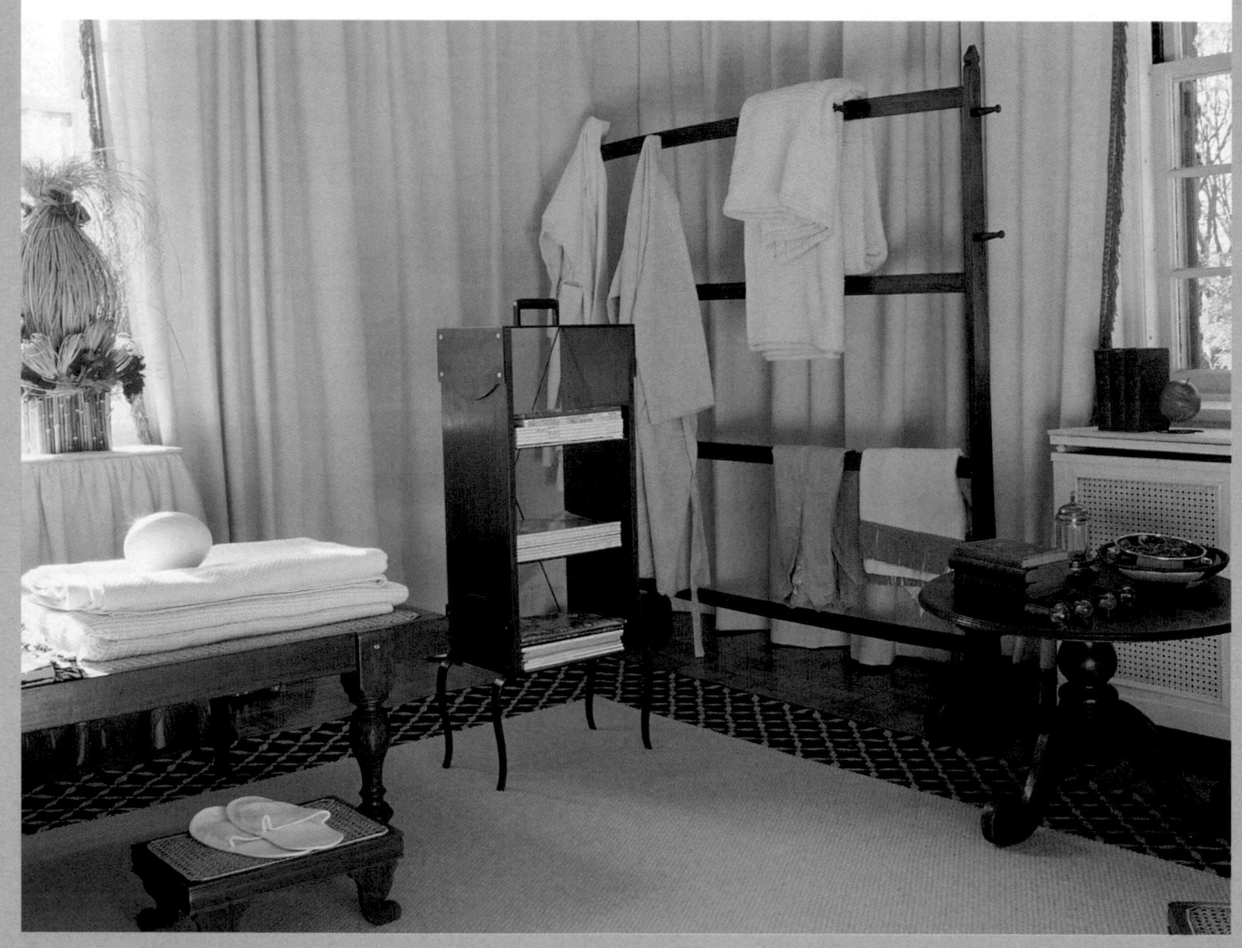

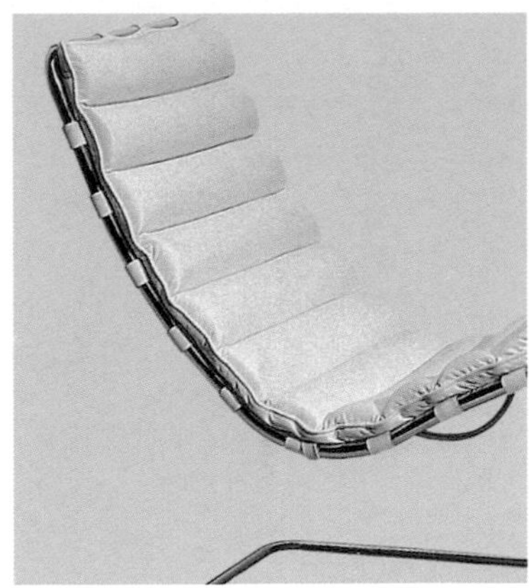

Furniture styles

Antique furniture is one of the keys to decoration. Gracefully bestowing style on a room is not as expensive as you may think. Going to an antique dealer can turn out to be quite costly because we end up having to pay for restoration. However, if we look around in secondhand markets we are likely to come across some surprising finds at reasonable prices.

Styles

A quick rundown of different styles will help us to choose furniture that is right for the ambience we are trying to create:

Baroque. Baroque furniture is characterized by being extravagantly ornamental, often with engraved figures and curved edges. It dates from the end of the seventeenth century and the beginning of the eighteenth. Two of the most important furniture manufacturers and woodcarvers of the period were Daniel Marot and Andrea Brustolon.

Queen Anne of England. This restrained, elegant furniture was principally made out of walnut wood, and it dates from the reign of Queen Anne (1702–1714). Some traits characteristic of the style are cabriole (curved, tapering) legs and vase-shaped back supports on the chairs.

Rococo. This French term refers to a spin-off of baroque style but lighter, more imaginative, and more playful. Ornaments were asymmetrical with motifs such as shells, foliage, and flowers. It began in France in about 1720. However, it is also found in England where it received the name "Chippendale."

Louis XV. This style is associated with curved silhouettes and asymmetrical shapes. The rococo style reached its peak during the reign of Louis XV (1715–1775) when people began to appreciate comfort. Chinese and oriental influences can be seen in this type of furniture.

Neoclassicism. This originated in the late eighteenth century as a result of the discovery of the Pompeii and Herculaneum remains. This caught the public's imagination, reviving interest in classical Greece. Classical motifs were soon being imitated on columns, garlands, and masks. This style of furniture is renowned for its elegance and lightness. The symmetry, frequent shallowness of relief, and

If we are after dramatic effects and want to add personality to a space, antique furniture is effective.

The classic forms and straight lines of the Louis XVI style create a restrained, conservative, yet somewhat overbearing style.

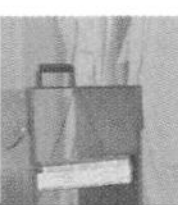

A regency sideboard or a modernist armchair add a touch of distinction to any room while at the same time serving as the central focus of a room.

straight lines are also identifying traits. Robert Adams was an important theorist of the neoclassic style and his designs, together with those of Hepplewhite and Sheratonson, are well-known.

Louis XVI. The straight lines of this style make it contrast with the Louis XV. The chair backs are oval-shaped; the legs straight, narrow, and fluted. Plated furniture came into fashion in this period (1774–1792), as did marquetry (wood inlay work), exotic wood, and laquer. The Louis XVI style was part of the Neoclassic movement and principally coincides with this king's reign, which ended with the French revolution. The chief artisans producing this type of furniture were Georges Jacob, Jean François Oeben, and Jean-Henri Riesener.

Regency. This term is used to designate the furniture created during the reign of the Prince of Wales (1811–1820). However, it is also applies to the period from 1790 to 1830. Inspired by classicism, its forms are heavier and more restrained than the neoclassic movement and it was characterized by decorative motifs from Rome, Greece, and Ancient Egypt. It should not be confused with French *régence* which was a pre-rococo style. The principal regency designers were Thomas Hope, George Smith, and Henry Holland.

Imperial. This is the French equivalent of the regency style and took place while Napoleon was in power (1804–1815). It is typified by its clean lines, minimal decoration, and absence of marquetry and carving. The decoration often includes work in metal, swans, military motifs, eagles, trophies, and Napoleonic emblems. The principal designer was Charles Percier.

Victorian. This term refers to furniture designed during the reign of Queen Victoria of England (1837-1901). It offers a mixture of neogothic, rococo, and neoclassic forms. Victorian decoration is usually very elaborate, and has a lot of carvings, inlaying, and metalwork. It is harsh. The furniture from the end of this period was influenced by the English arts and crafts movement and the French art nouveau.

Art nouveau. This French style, dating from the beginning of the twentieth century, is characterized by the innovative interpretation of ancient decorative forms, standing out especially the floral ornamentation and references to nature. While this movement was happening in France,

The decorative possibilities of antique furniture and lamps are sure to surprise us. Just a few elements are sufficient to create classy ambiences.

Catalan Modernism and its curved forms were catching on across the southern border, although the two movements are aesthetically different.

Arts and crafts. This movement originated in England as a response to the Industrial Revolution at the end of the nineteenth century. It tended heavily toward artisanal elaboration, economic and straightforward design, and shunned superfluous decoration. It brought traditional techniques back into fashion. William Morris (1834–1896) was one of its leading designers, as was Charles R. Mackintosh, although the two men's furniture displays some differences in style.

Thonet. The late nineteenth-century German designer Micheal Thonet not only produced curved wood furniture; he also came up with a way of manufacturing it in batches. Many of his chairs, manufactured in Europe and America, are still valued today.

Twentieth-century designers. Throughout the twentieth century different architects and designers have produced valuable furniture that can be defined as art. To name them all would take up too much space so we will concentrate on the most influential. Charles Eames, an American designer, was best-known for the beauty, comfort, elegance, and delicacy of his mass-producible chairs and leather armchairs, still the rage today. The French architect Le Corbusier designed a chaise longue out of tubular steel in 1927 and an armchair known as the Grand Comfort. Miles van der Rohe came up with the well-known Barcelona armchair. Alvar Aalto turned out curved back plywood chairs. Arne Jacobsen, Marcel Breuer, and Carl Jacobs also left their mark.

 How to combine styles

When we are dealing with furniture the whole collection must take precedence over individual pieces. It is easy to fall under the spell of an antique piece of furniture, but we have to consider how it will fit in with everything else. And, of course, we have to ask ourselves whether it meets our needs.

Antique objects, covered in a beautiful luster from the passing of time, become more engaging as they grow old.

Everybody loves to buy new things, but before bringing in new furniture we must figure out whether we can take advantage of what we already have. We may want to restore or renovate the external appearance of furniture if it is shabby or drab. Decorating is not merely throwing out the old and bringing in new objects. Moreover, although new furniture is certainly attractive—not to mention pricey—if we were to search secondhand markets and antique dealers, we would probably come across some surprising pieces of furniture that add a touch of distinction to our home. Remember that old furniture has more personality than new designs and can be a source of inspiration as we seek to create our own atmosphere. Old furniture is sufficiently interesting to be the central feature of a room but be sure never to mix antique furniture of different styles.

Hodgepodge does look good but you have to be a creative genius to get it right; otherwise, a room could end up looking like an antique dealer's showroom. It is a risk we should avoid. The general rule is that if we have one very characteristic piece of antique furniture, the other, more restrained pieces, should stay out of the limelight. In bigger rooms we can place two or three pieces of antique furniture without overdoing it.

TEN HELPFUL HINTS

1 If there is a special piece of antique furniture in the room it will probably become the central feature, so organize according to it.

2 Restoring, stripping, or painting a piece of antique furniture can give it a new lease on life.

3 Reupholstering chairs, armchairs, or sofas is an economical way of renovating furniture.

4 Movable furniture on wheels and foldable chairs and tables are ideal for small, multifunctional spaces.

5 Furniture can be used strategically to divide up spaces and create different ambiences.

6 Architecturally provocative spaces should be furnished with clean, crisp-line furniture.

7 When choosing furniture, analyze which pieces are really necessary and which can be done away with.

8 Auxiliary tables, like coffee tables, are vital for multipurpose rooms.

9 Use an antique piece of furniture for inspiration or as the starting point when appropriate.

10 Use furniture to link the different rooms in the house together.

We should consider restoring old furniture or giving a new lease on life to dull elements with little dashes of color or other personal details.

MATERIALS

Fabrics

Just like paint, fabric is usable in various ways. It can allow us to change the look of a room and furniture fairly easily. Traditionally it was used to cover walls but has since given way to wallpaper, which is more practical and easy to use while carrying out the same function.

The biggest contribution of fabric is curtains, which stand out due to their size. Be careful when choosing a pattern because you will probably only have a sample of the material to help you imagine how it will look full-size and in the context of the room. The same problem applies when choosing fabric for tapestries, sofas, armchairs, and chair upholstery.

The tendency to decorate the whole room in the same fabric is fading away. It is now quite common to find decorations based on color ranges. Many possibilities are available in decorating shops, making the work even easier by selling fabrics and papers in the same pattern. With imagination and inspiration, we will be able to come up with appealing schemes.

The textures of fabrics vary but all of them add warmth and personality to a room. Another advantage is that they absorb noise—a plus when we have problems with sound insulation.

Curtains allow us to filter light and to create a cozier ambience. Combining sofas with different patterns enriches the space.

A fabric's texture can make a room warmer and more snug while at the same time allowing us to modify the look of the furniture.

Coverings

Coverings is the name given to all the materials used to cover, protect, or decorate ceilings and walls. Nearly all types of materials—stone, plaster, fabrics, paper, wood, stucco—can be used to cover or clad the walls and ceilings. The market offers endless possibilities to solve any problem that may come up while decorating.

When choosing the wall coverings for the ground floor we have to make sure that there are no humidity problems. If there are, we should consult an expert who can tell us how serious the problem is and what steps must be taken. The other house walls normally do not require special treatment, except the bathroom and possibly the kitchen. If any walls suffer the direct action of water, or greasy fumes around the stove, we will choose a suitably resistant material, probably marble, stainless steel—contemporary and sleek—or tiles. The rule that wood should not be used near dampness or where it can get splashed no longer holds true due to improved waterproofing techniques. However, constant wetting would be a problem in the long run.

The wall covering chosen for each space is determined not only by the style and ambience we wish to create but also by practical aspects such as maintenance. Paint must be recoated periodically as it gets dirty easily. However, there are now washable paints, even water-based ones especially suitable for children's rooms. Tiles do not stand up to wear and tear; they get chipped and do not allow us to drill holes. It is worth looking into the new solutions coming on to the market, like stucco work and stone tiles. Think about how a material will look next to the surrounding decoration materials while trying to imagine the sample at full size. Special care is necessary before going ahead with installation of a the wall covering because normally it is a quite costly process and difficult to change.

Floorings

The factors to be taken into account when deciding on the floor are quite similar to those for the wall coverings. In this case, however, the surface area is smaller but the practical considerations are more important. What kind of use are we going to give to the space? Heavy use requires resistant materials, especially if people are constantly walking back and forth in dirty shoes. The floor must stand up to scuffing. The coldness or warmth of flooring depends on a room's ambience. Wooden boards are often used in bedrooms because they feel good on bare feet, but carpet (comfy and soothing) and tiles with under-floor heating also give a pleasant sensation. Make sure the flooring matches the wall coverings and once again when looking at the material sample try to imagine how it will look full scale. Our capacity to imagine and extrapolate is crucial for good decoration.

Getting the flooring right requires a capacity to imagine the finished effect under lighting.

Consider the possibility of playing flooring against carpets and rugs. The latter add warmth and comfort to a home.

DO

If you want to combine different patterns, bear in mind that they should have colors in common to link them together.

Using tough floorings for heavily used spaces is recommended.

Combine fabrics and wallpaper around the house to give it a sense of unity.

Use fabrics to soundproof rooms that have bad acoustics.

DO NOT

Combine different fabric patterns in small or cluttered rooms.

Use materials such as wood for flooring, or fabric on the walls in rooms such as the bathroom where water may get splashed about.

Wallpaper large rooms with a plain or repetitive pattern. For such rooms it is better to combine styles or to use paint.

Use large floor tiles or boards in small rooms. Similarly, using small floor pieces should be avoided in large rooms.

In the kitchen and bathrooms it is important to install flooring that stands up to spills while still combining well with the furniture.

PASTA

One of the biggest factors to be considered when choosing the floor material is the use given to a room.

TEN HELPFUL HINTS

1 Use fabrics to provide soundproofing in noisy rooms.

2 Curtains or blinds allow us to play with light.

3 Choose flooring according to a room´s use.

4 Use warm floorings like carpets or wood where you will walk barefoot.

5 Use tough floorings like marble, stone, or tiles where lots of people move about, especially if they have hard heels or dirty soles.

6 Before choosing flooring, try and determine how it will look in the lighting of a room.

7 Take good care of your flooring to ensure it will last a long time.

8 Avoid paint in areas with heavy circulation. Tiles and marble are both washable and longer-lasting.

9 When deciding on the flooring and the wall coverings remember just how much space they occupy and therefore how important they are.

10 Well-matched wall coverings and floorings can be mutually enhancing so it is best to select them at the same time.

COMPLEMENTS

The importance of complements

As soon as we start decorating, and not just planning, we will realize that the little details are usually what give a room its style and mood.

Details speak volumes about the personality and tastes of the person who chooses them. Decoration is a process of creating a pleasing space using diverse techniques and resources, the final stage of which is applying the little details. Sometimes just by changing little things the room takes on a surprisingly different look. However, this does not mean we should get carried away and fill the space up with all kinds of objects that catch our fancy.

The details that will make our home feel like a place we can call our own should be selected carefully over time, without rushing. Some of them will be keepsakes—and these are not found every day. We can get ideas by leafing through books, seeing what catches our eye and fits in with our lifestyle.

 Candles

Candles are decorative elements that seemed to have been forgotten but are once again popular in contemporary interior design. Not only are candles beautiful, coming in various shapes and pretty colors, but they also provide lighting which makes you feel good in a way that electric lighting rarely does.

Candles provide light. They add warmth and ambience to a room. They are a nice theatrical touch.

Candles can illuminate a room and give a warm feeling of well-being that artificial light will never match.

Candles are suitable for everyday activities. You need not wait for a special occasion to put them on the dining table. Their glow and flickering flames will warm the spirits of any social group and encourage relaxed conversation. For family get togethers and on special occasions candles are a must. They bring people together while enjoying good food and conversation. Of course, they are also good in other rooms besides the dining room. In the bathroom, their tenuous light is a perfect mood creator. They encourage us to linger, letting the water and mineral salts soak away our stress. Though they are not the best light to read by, they do invite us to stretch out and unwind in our most intimate room, our bedroom. On calm days, candles are even suitable for making the garden or balcony more enchanting.

Scented candles will fill our home with a sweet aroma. Some fragrances are good for our health: decoration is not only concerned with aesthetics. An ambience that helps us to escape the hectic pace of life can be invaluable.

It is easy to get used to candles in everyday life, especially on occasions such as family meals when they are an integral part of table decoration, or lighting up corners.

DO

Take advantage of the decorative qualities of candles to illuminate spaces lacking natural light.

Use candles as decorative objects on special occasions such as meals with family and friends.

Burn scented candles to fill the house with soft fragrance.

DON'T

Place candles where children can reach them or near flammable fabrics.

Leave candles burning when you are not at home.

Place candles at eye level because they can be blinding or bothersome.

Objects, details, and complements say a lot about the people who chose them, so be careful where and how you use them.

Plants

Modern cities separate us from the natural beauty of the country and have obliged us to change our lifestyle. Land is now too expensive for most people to have gardens, and instead inner city flats are full of plants. If we are really lucky we will have a terrace where we can grow plants that need outdoor conditions. We can have a few carefully chosen plants indoors and a terrace filled with vitality, color, and fragrance.

Plants remind us that humans need to be in contact with nature. They attempt to make up for the lack of a traditional garden.

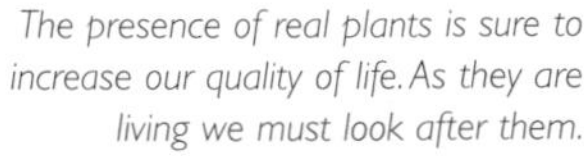

The presence of real plants is sure to increase our quality of life. As they are living we must look after them.

Complements

Plants are living, and growing and in return for breathing life and freshness into our homes, they have to be looked after. Some plants, such as cacti, are standard decorative elements but our choices aren't limited to these. As always, go for what you like and what fits in with the ambience you are trying to create. Before taking a plant home from the garden center, remember that it is alive and will grow, both vertically and horizontally. The specialists will inform you about the best species, and colors, and how to take care of them and what living conditions they need. Besides plants, simple flower arrangements look good despite being relatively short-lived. Their freshness cannot be matched by any other decorative element.

DO

Choose plants taking into consideration the conditions in which they will be kept.

Place growing plants near sunlight and natural ventilation.

Use plants as a substitute for not having a traditional garden. They are decorative elements which introduce nature into our home.

DO NOT

Put plants near heat sources like radiators.

Use natural plants in bedrooms.

Neglect plants. As they are alive and growing, look after them properly.

Dried flowers

Some people do not have sufficient time to look after natural plants but are not prepared to go without their beauty. The solution they often come up with are dried flowers. Their charm is similar to that of natural plants, though less changeable and less vivid. Their shades may be different from that of growing plants or blooming flowers but they are still magical. Green leaves and brightly colored petals turn into all sorts of fantastic, less intense but still resplendent tones. They are perfect for placing in the center of a dining table, remaining intact over time. Do not limit yourself to standard arrangements—experiment with new ones.

Dried flowers allow us to savor the beauty of nature when a room does not offer adequate conditions—sunlight and fresh air—for a living plant.

We can change the look of a dried flower arrangement often. The decoration must evolve with us and our moods.

DO

Use dried plants and flowers in rooms without the necessary conditions for living ones.

Clean them and look after them often to preserve them over time.

Give them a fresh look every now and then by changing the position of the branches or the vase they are in.

DON'T

Use dried flowers as a substitute for natural plants.

Buy a bunch of dried flowers without bearing in mind how they match up with the color scheme.

Architectural features

The term architectural features refers to the structure of a building and the possibilities it offers for our interior design project. It is what we find when we start a project or the makeover. Architectural features enhance interior spaces and make them more interesting. Sometimes we can create our own architectural features to help us even up a space or to make it more charismatic. For example, we may find a column that throws the composition of a room off balance. Unable to knock it down, we can add another one to restore equilibrium. Cornices, ceiling roses, and other elements in plaster help us to create the period setting we are seeking. If we have to decorate a room that is short on natural light we can create a false window illuminated artificially from behind. However, the best solution is to make an opening (in an internal wall) and borrow light coming in through the windows. This little trick makes the ambience less dull and gives the sensation that the room is connected to the outside. However, this "deconstructing," or reconstructing, of our home is an option that should be used carefully.

A staircase, a skylight, or a glass ceiling are architectural features that give a lot of individuality to a room.

The architectural features themselves can be decorative elements and must therefore match the tone set by the rest of the decoration.

The architecture of a house presents endless ways of creating a space that expresses our personality

TEN HELPFUL HINTS

1 A double-height space allows us to link different ambiences and to improve natural lighting.

2 Before modifying an architectural feature we should analyze thoroughly how it affects the other features.

3 A cornice in the upper part of the wall or on the ceiling can be used to unify spaces.

4 A window or a door can be emphasized by surrounding it with a cornice.

5 A ceiling rose in the middle of the room balances the composition and enriches the decoration.

6 In dreary spaces we can create an artificial window illuminated from behind.

7 A dropped ceiling enables us to modify the dimensions of a room that has too much space overhead.

8 If there is a column that throws everything out of balance, we can create a false one to match.

9 Architectural features such as cornices, ceiling roses, and pediments are essential if we want to create a classic ambience.

10 We can turn architectural features into part of the furniture: wall-mounted tables, ledges, and half-height walls are examples.

Architectural features such as cornices and ceiling roses offer the possibility of enriching the room and creating dramatic ambiences.

Materials

"I want to live with the same sincerity with which I construct. I have destroyed many beautiful things in the hope of being able to substitute them with other things even more beautiful."

Frank Lloyd Wright

FABRICS

curtains • upholstery • carpets

Fabrics

Perhaps we do not always know how to appreciate and take advantage of the decorative capacity of fabrics. Not only are they economical, but they also allow us to change the look and mood of a room. Take the case of a chair or sofa cover. Along with the aesthetic possibilities of the color and texture of a furniture cover, the way in which a cover is attached can also subtly influence the mood. It can be attached with ribbons for a romantic look, or strapped down with leather for a stately ambience. Straight lined fabric patterns make furniture look modern and functional. To what extent we utilize the charm of fabrics is in our hands.

A whole range of opportunities are opened up by the use of fabrics, only limited by our imagination and creativity. We can use them in a traditional way as table cloths, bedspreads and sheets, curtains and tapestries, or we can go further and convert functional objects into elements of decoration.

Curtains

Any type of fabric can be used for curtains, from silk or lace to thick, coarse cloth. If we use fine materials and we find that they do not filter light sufficiently, we can use a second, purely functional curtain.

Curtains must fit in with the rest of the ambience, maintaining a room's balance. Since any type of fabric is suitable for a curtain, we should choose according to how much we want to spend and the style we are seeking. The curtain fabric should be twice the width of the window. Natural smooth fabrics give a fresh, modern feel. Silks are delicate and romantic. Patterned baizes and felts are good for period pieces. Hessian and sacking recall country houses. The way the curtain is attached to the bar is just as important as the fabric used. These little details must not be neglected if the total design is to be effective.

Window shades

Roller blinds

Venetian blinds

Sheer curtains

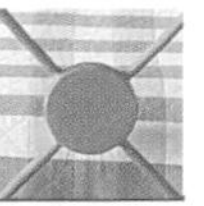

 Window shades

Very much in vogue over recent years, window shades are practical decorative elements in line with today's aesthetics. They can be used alone or combined with other curtains. Bars sewn into the fabric allow them to move up and down (curtains are normally opened by pulling them to both sides of the window), controlled by a cord pulley system. They can be bought by the square yard, in any shape, though they are also available in standard measurements and basic colors. Despite being more complicated to make (a specialist has to do it) they are inexpensive because they use less fabric.

When folded, the pattern loses its effect, so it should not be too big. Bear this in mind when buying the fabric. Window shades, totally contemporary, are very practical window coverings because they allow the amount of light coming in to be controlled horizontally.

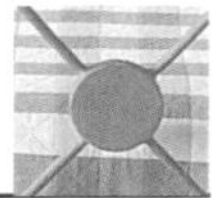

Window shades determine the quality of the light coming in. Patterns can be combined if we use discretion.

DO

Combine fabrics with the same tone, whether they have a pattern or are plain.

In small spaces we can use roller blinds or window shades since they take up less space and foster the illusion of having more room.

In rooms with large windows, combine different types of curtains—net, lace, window shades—to provide variety and liven up a room visually.

DO NOT

Decorate a small room with a multitude of patterns and color shades. This would make it feel smaller and untidy.

Use large patterns to make shades. When folded away you cannot see them. Instead, combine very distinct patterns in different tones.

Combine fabrics where either the tones or the pattern aren't similar.

Roller blinds

Very similar to window shades, roller blinds are based on a simple system. Plain fabric is rolled up either above or below the window and lowered down, or raised up by a cord pulley system. They are very useful because, similar to sheer curtains, they let softened light through but can preserve your privacy. They are also height adjustable. They are available in standard sizes or can be made to measure. Traditionally, roller blinds always rolled down, but today modern models are on the market that allow the coil to be at the bottom, like a screen.

Very similar looking to window shades, roller blinds can be stored away either above or below the window, allowing us to control where the light enters or to maintain privacy.

Venetian blinds

Venetian blinds have overlapping horizontal slats. The amount of light that enters can be controlled by either pulling the slats up altogether, leaving the window totally clear, or by twisting the slats so that they are horizontal and let in a lot of light. This type of composition provides good aesthetics and enhances the windows.

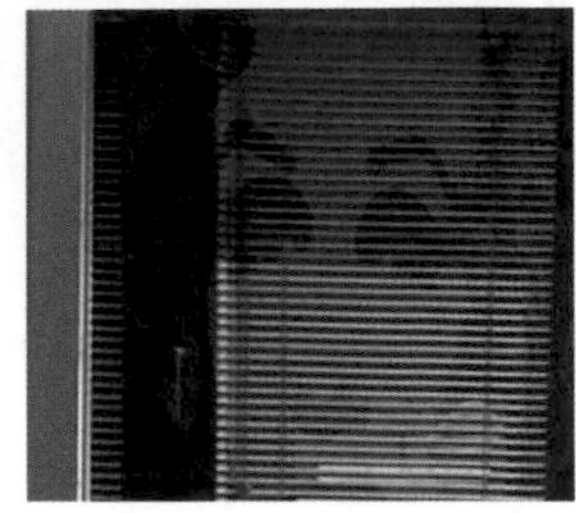

Venetian blinds allow the quantity of light let in to be adjusted by inclining the slats or by pulling them up and letting them down.

Their modern look, along with their practicality, mean that venetian blinds work well in uncluttered, simple lined spaces. They can also be placed between panes of double glazing and will then be protected from dirt.

Sheer curtains

Fine fabrics such as gauze, muslin, batiste, or even shiny fabrics such as silk or organdy, can be used to make sheer curtains that filter the light without actually blocking it completely. Alternatively, they can be used for exclusively decorative purposes to give a romantic, cozy air to the room. Colored sheer curtains give new shades of light and create a special ambience. Sheer curtains can hang loose like drapes or they can be given structure by hanging on a frame.

Curtains and sheer curtains are very effective as drapes.

The principal function of net curtains is to filter light, giving a room special ambience.

Upholstery

Upholstery is an affordable way of giving a fresh long-lasting and hard-wearing look to furniture. Before throwing away old furniture we must decide if we would be better off refinishing it. What is cheap is not automatically distasteful. If we are not sure whether to reupholster or to buy a new chair or sofa, a temporary solution is to put a blanket or rug over the worn out upholstery. However, sooner or later we will have to come up with a permanent solution.

Upholstery makes a room feel warmer; it changes the look of furniture in a simple way, and still allows you to stay within your budget.

Good quality fabrics for upholstery are normally expensive. However, suppliers are happy to offer a wide range of styles, in all price ranges. Work out the exact quantity of fabric needed to avoid waste. You can tell the fabric quality by its weight. The heavier it is, the longer it will last. Fabrics can also be tested by rubbing. When decorating with fabrics you need not follow strict furniture conventions. A certain amount of improvisation is possible. If you try out materials not expressly designed for upholstery, bear in mind that you may have problems with creases and folds.

Chair and sofa covers offer the possibility of changing the look of the furniture and the room. Period upholstery is effective for creating a classic ambience.

Choosing a color or a pattern for fabric is important. Not only must it match the curtains, but it also must team up with the furniture, the flooring, and the walls. If you are afraid of getting it wrong, you can opt for natural tones, particularly beiges and grays, which go well with all colors. If we are keen on patterns, neutral tone stripes are practical in all spaces, with all styles and for all ambiences. Apart from decorative effects, we also have to consider the furniture's function and the treatment it will receive. Children going through the "rough and tumble" age take their toll on fabrics. Darker hues need less washing, and some fabrics are even dirt repellent and stain-proof. Sofas near fireplaces should be covered in non-flammable materials. Furniture in the open air will have to be covered with fabrics which stand up to humidity and the fading effects of sunlight.

Specialists can help us choose the best upholstery material for our necessities. Silk is so fine that it is impractical. Cotton, linen, and light wool are suitable as furniture covers because they are washable, although they are not very long-lasting. Indian cotton, velvet, and brushed nankeen are firm, durable fabrics that give good results. Generally, the thicker and more closely woven a fabric is, and the more body it has, the better it stands up to wear and the passing of time.

To give a personal touch to furniture covers we can sew on buttons or beads. The cushion patterns can break the monotony of the space, but be careful: there is a fine line between flouting the rules and bad taste. If for you beauty is color, patterns and fabrics offer a great opportunity not to have to play it safe, while still creating a harmonious space.

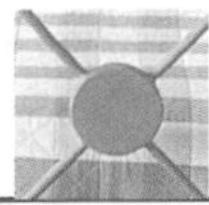

A fabric pattern can be turned into the central feature of a space, organizing the rest of the decoration around it.

Combining fabrics gives a room distinction.

Carpets

Carpets open up endless decoration possibilities for converting a cold, hard stone floor into a warm, comfortable surface you will love walking across. Carpets are ideal for defining spaces in a living area and for creating different ambiences around the house, from the foyer clear through to the landing. At informal get-togethers, when the sofas are full, you can stretch out on them. Or when alone you can lie down in front of the television to watch your favorite program. Besides being soft and comfortable, they are also casually elegant. It is a myth that carpets will always exceed your budget. Prices for kilims or carpets hand woven in Nepal are high, but good carpets can also be found at affordable prices.

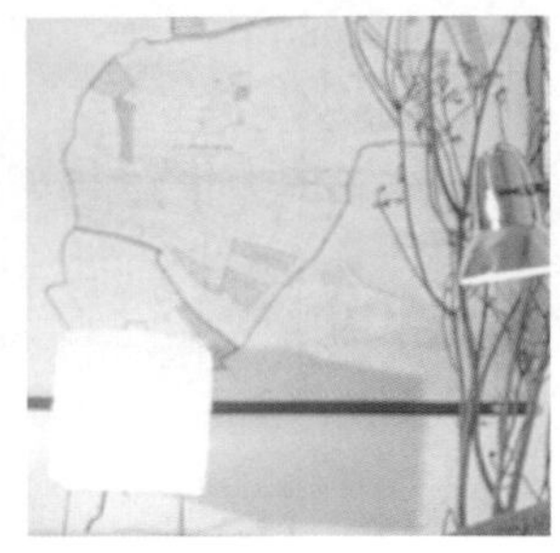

Carpets are hard-wearing and adaptable to different spaces. When you want to rearrange a house a little you can put them in other rooms or even take them with you if you move. They must be properly fitted on a level floor and not creased up. If the flooring underneath is slippery, tack them down on top of a rubber mat.

Work with the colors of carpets to stimulate interest in the decoration.

A brief rundown of the different types of carpets and styles available will give us an idea as to which one will best suit our needs.

Oriental carpets. Woven in wool and silk, these thick, richly artistic carpets come in a wide palette of colors, yellow, black, peach, or pastel pink. Though they originated in China, today they are imported from other Asian countries such as India. Make sure that the manufacturer is not exploiting children.

Kilims are made in Iran, Iraq, China, Pakistan, India, Russia, and Morocco. The designs on kilims are like trademarks for the different tribes and there is an array of motifs and explosive colors. They are relatively hard carpets and tend to be long rather than wide.

Persian rugs, characterized by fine warp and filling yarns and a tight, even pile made with the Sehna knot, are found in rectangular and elongated shapes. Blue and red are the principal colors. They become more alluring as they age.

***Bujara* or *turkmena*.** Carpets are easily recognizable because of their geometric, repetitive patterns. Woven in Afghanistan, Pakistan, and Turkmenistan, they are not tough and therefore are unsuitable for heavy wear on a regular basis. However, they are great for introducing fine detail into a room.

***Dhurrie* carpets** are fringed, usually rectangular cotton carpets manufactured in India. They are more suitable in summer than winter.

Other less well-known types of carpets can also be found, like the carpets from the Caucasian mountains with their vivid colors and child-like patterns. Patchwork carpets are made by joining together lots of little pieces. Greek flokati carpets are hairy and heavy. Rya carpets are from Scandinavian countries (Norway, Finland, and Sweden) and have frayed edges. Sarape rugs are blankets from Mexico or Turkey, crafted by artisans and becoming more appreciated as time goes by.

Combining the tones of the carpet with the curtains and walls can unify a room.

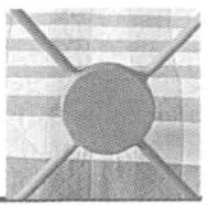

DO

Use the carpets to make spaces with cold floors warmer and more comfortable.

Cover heavily trafficked floors that are delicate with carpets. They are easy on your feet, while at the same time protecting the floor surface.

Choose curtain design and texture according to the style we are seeking and our practical necessities.

DO NOT

Go too far combining patterns, upholstery, and carpets that overload a room with a mish-mash of colors and textures.

Plan and choose fabrics out of context. The results will not be coherent.

Use delicate fabrics for upholstering heavily used sofas.

A colorful, fun carpet sends out a confident message and lightens up a neutral space.

des années 50 ...
rencontre
L'AMÉRIQUE
des années 90 !
J.D.

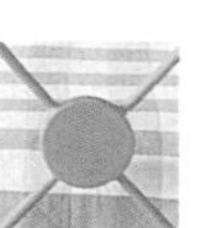

Carpets are basically associated with protecting flooring. However, there is no reason why they should not be draped over a banister or hung on a wall.

Small patterned rugs are ideal for spaces dominated by straight simple lines.

TEN HELPFUL HINTS

1 Match curtain fabrics with upholstery to unify spaces that seem untidy.

2 Use carpets to mark off spaces. A rug is ideal for establishing a social zone within a room.

3 Fabrics with classic patterns give a period feeling to the ambience of a room.

4 Remember that the bedlinen, tablecloths, and towels also contribute to decoration.

5 Sheer curtains and gauze enable us to filter light.

6 Venetian blinds allow control over the amount of light entering a room.

7 Do not limit curtains and blinds to just windows. The former can be used in an excessively long passage or hallway. Blinds make good screens.

8 In rooms with a lot of pictures, different colored walls, or furniture, it is advisable to use neutral tones for the curtains and upholstery.

9 Take advantage of fabrics by using them to renovate your furniture.

10 Use rugs and tapestries as hangings on a wall. Their color and texture are unbeatable and they improve acoustics.

FLOORINGS

wood floors • hard floors • textile floors

Floorings

Many types of materials can be used to cover the floor. Although walls (discussed further later) have a larger surface area, floors are just as important because we actually come into physical contact with them constantly and therefore they directly influence how comfortable we are.

Choosing the right floor is complicated, and there are many types of material that are suitable for the different functions of flooring. As always, practicality, budget, and ambience come into play: go for the most practical material that best suits your needs, is not too hard on your pocket, and fits in with the style in the rest of the house, and more particularly the ambience you are trying to attain. The weight of some floors mean they need sturdy support beams and are not thus suitable for old or unsteady building structures. Also bear in mind that different flooring materials will inevitably come into contact with each other at some point, a problem that can be tricky to resolve. Try to make sure that there are not too many seams in the corridor or foyer. Getting round the problem of unsightly seams should be taken into consideration when deciding on the flooring.

Wood floors

Wood, one of the oldest materials used in construction, comes from what was once a living tree and therefore has special characteristics other materials do not have. The varied textures and colors available open up a wide range of possibilities.

Wood ages, gaining dignity over time. If well cared for it can remain strong for many years. Indeed, we sometimes wish to take advantage of the nobility wood acquires over the years due to its beautiful luster.

Wood is characterized by its color, texture, grain (the direction in which the fibers of the board rise to the surface), and knots. The range of varieties available on the market is wide: rosewood, boards, plywood, and even some very convincing knockoffs.

The size of the pieces of wood is also significant in creating the style for the room. Small, mosaic pieces give an intimate feel to the room, while larger planks or boards produce a sensation of spaciousness.

If you want to use wood in your home, your options are limited as to how you can treat it. Before going ahead with your decoration plan, try out the different finishes obtained with small samples. Wood can be lacquered, pro-

A wooden floor warms the room up in a way few materials can match.

Parquet

Floorboards

Mosaic

Wood finishes

tected with oil, painted, varnished, or stained. The base color of the wood will show through any varnish or stain we apply to it. Because of their nature, some woods must be treated gently. The sun tends to bleach wood so do not expose it to direct sunlight. Leaving heavy furniture on the same spot of floor could cause indentations so spread the weight a little (and use coasters).

Wood requires care in a way that other materials do not. This disadvantage is more than compensated for by its natural ornamental surface, alluring luster, and aromatic scent.

As a floor surface wood has the advantage of being neither fully rigid nor fully flexible. It has good acoustics (it absorbs sound), but at the same time it makes its own noise, such as creaking, and footsteps. The sound of feet thumping across the floorboards above can be annoying for people below. However, this problem can be easily solved by covering the wood with sound absorbers such as a carpet with a layer of felt underneath.

Sturdy wood can be restored and will last for a long time, while plywood, which is cheaper, cannot be restored and has a shorter life span. We must always take into consideration that wood requires special care and should not be placed where it will have to stand up to natural forces (or elements) such as rain or sunshine. Put a doormat by the front door since dirty shoes could also ruin the gloss of a wood. Varnish must be reapplied periodically in order to maintain its protective qualities.

Wood is a tried and true classic suitable for decorating nearly the whole house. However, it requires regular upkeep if it is placed in rooms with humidity, such as the bathroom and the kitchen.

As wood comes from trees, it creates a cozy country look.

The soft-spoken good looks of wood mean that it has always been used in homes, regardless of design trends at the time of its installation. The drawback is that extra effort is required to ensure that spillage and humidity in the bathroom and the kitchen won't spoil it. However, some wood is tougher than we may think. Teak, a tropical hardwood, resists water rot and when covered with deck oil (found in hardware stores) ages with a beautiful orange glossiness.

Wood is sold ready to be installed after being dried out to ensure that it will not buckle or shift once in place. You cannot be too cautious; before actually fitting it into place in a bathroom or kitchen, just place it in that room for a couple of days. This way it can adapt to the conditions of the room and avoid shrinkage and swelling, or even cracking later on.

Wood tiles or boards can be laid out in a pattern created around the motif or shade of each element. The way tiles lay will lead our eyes across a room. In elongated rooms, placing boards parallel to the longest side will emphasize the length of the room even more. Perpendicular boards produce the opposite effect. Decoration allows us to put all these options to good use. For example, in a corridor we may wish to place the accent of the wood according to the 'traffic flow' and therefore fit the boards parallel to the long walls.

The surge in interest for ecological, natural materials has meant that wood has become increasingly fashionable. We must make sure that we do not use up unreplaceable natural resources, by importing tropical wood (mahogany, sapelly, teak and keruing) only from forests that can sustain the loss of trees. Some countries have forbidden the exportation of these products due to the abuse forests are suffering. Also, make sure that the products we use to treat the wood—such as fillers, oils, tints, and varnishes—are as natural as possible.

What wood looks like depends on how it is cut. Cutting against the grain makes the wood harder than when it is cut radially, though doing the latter gives it a more uniform finish as far as the grain is concerned. The strength of an individual piece depends on the direction in which weight is applied. A board is strongest along the grain (axially) but when bent it is strongest perpendicular to the grain (transversely). The third possibility, which is cheaper and more commonly practiced, is to saw it in a straight line. The setback to this is that the wood becomes lower in quality and less long-lasting.

Density is another variable in the process of choosing wood. The denser it is, the tougher it is at standing up to wear and tear and the passing of time. The most widely used woods come from two groups of trees: broadleaves, or hardwoods, which include such trees as oak, walnut, and maple; softwoods, or conifers, such as pine, spruce, or fir. Trees classified as hardwoods are not necessarily harder than softwoods. Balsa, for example, is a hardwood but is actually one of the softest woods. Rather, hardwoods and softwoods differ, in their cellular form and structure. The latter are cheaper and more abundant. The most common are fir trees and pine wood. Nowadays hardwoods are more prominent and it is therefore easier to find a wide range of them in the market, with different finishes, textures, and motifs.

The most widely used woods are the following:

Beechwood: This light-colored wood is tough and long-lasting.

Ashtree: This is another light-colored wood with a rough texture and irregular shapes.

Maple: This reddish wood stands up very well to the wear and tear of everyday use.

Oak: This irregularly grained wood is tough and long-lasting. It is popular because of its resistance to humidity and rotting.

There are other less well-known and not so commonly used types of woods. Birchwood is light-colored and has a delicate texture. Chestnut is tough and long-lasting. Cherrywood has a reddish hue and a fine grain. Wood from the linden tree has a straight grain; it is soft and whitish. Walnut has a wavy grain. Elm is dark and resilient. The wood of the sycamore tree is light-colored. Pinewood is soft and lightweight, not too sturdy but heavily used because it is affordable.

Light-colored woods like birch brighten up a room.

DO

Choose the type of wood used according to its function and the room it will be in.

Analyze how it should be fitted. It must be compatible with decoration and ambience.

Treat wood with preservatives if it is going to be subject to adverse conditions, such as humidity or direct sunlight.

DO NOT

Overuse wood by placing it on floors, walls, or ceiling unless it is suitable for the style we are creating.

Use wood in spaces where tough conditions will take their toll.

Choose small wood floor boards or tiles that are inappropriate for decorating large spaces. Long, wide, wooden floor strips are more adequate.

Wood is not only available as it comes off the tree. Technology has generated woods such as plywood, a laminated panel made of a wood core glued between layers of veneer. The grain of each layer in plywood runs in opposite directions, and different types of wood can be used. Resins can be added to protect the wood. Another option is particleboard or chipboard. This is made by gluing chunks, shaving, and splinters of wood together.

Fibreboard is a panel formed from wood-pulp fibers. Today plywood, fiberboard, and particleboard are increasingly used and varnished over like natural wood. The most commonly used manufactured woods are made with leftovers of small pieces of wood. Mixtures with bigger chunks give a rich and attractive texture.

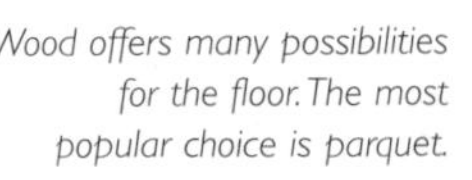

Wood offers many possibilities for the floor. The most popular choice is parquet.

Parquet

Although it is now very much the craze, parquet was also very widely used in the French palaces of the seventeenth and eighteenth centuries.There are several simple variations in the way parquet can be laid, a few of them are complicated and specially suitable for certain design ideas.

They can be placed in a simple line, or more complex forms like rhombuses, motifs, or friezes.A specialist in a hardware store will tell us how to get the most out of what we buy. The finished effect not only depends on the type of wood used, but also on the size of the tiles and how they are laid.

Fortunately, as the traditional laying method for parquet requires a professional, there are simpler systems available in do-it-yourself stores that can be installed by just about anyone who has basic home repair skills. This chipboard parquet comes ready to fit and does not require the floor base to be prepared beforehand.

Hardwoods are normally used for parquet, though sometimes pine is used.

The traditional process for laying parquet is laborious and should be carried out by a specialist if we want to get all the beauty out of wood.

DO	DO NOT
Treat parquet with special oils when it is placed in bathrooms or kitchens.	*Install parquet where it will be directly exposed to dirty shoes or hard heels. It can be scratched.*
Use wide, long tiles in big spaces and smaller tiles for more modest rooms.	*Use parquet on flooring constantly subject to humidity.*
Leave a little space between each tile to prevent warping when the wood swells (this happens naturally).	*Use parquet in spaces where people are always coming and going. If it has already been laid, protect it with a rug.*

Floorboards

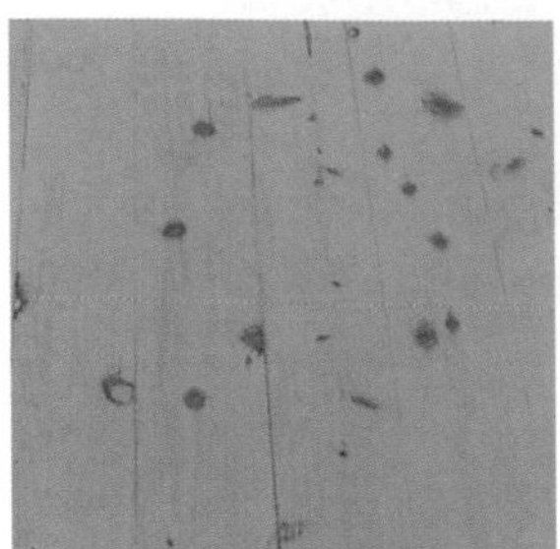

The process used for laying floorboards is very similar to that used for parquet but the final result can be very different. Floorboards can vary in both length and width: the bigger they are, the more expensive they will be. The boards can range in thickness from $1/4$ inch to 1 inch. Thin boards cannot be restored because this requires polishing them in such a way that a thin layer is taken off the top. We also have to make sure that the bolts are not affected by this "sanding." Wide floorboards are more aesthetically pleasing but often, they are not the most appropriate in a cramped space because they may lose their charm. In the market there are prefabricated solutions that are economical and easy to lay down.

Wooden floorboards produce a linear sensation in a room. They are ideal for drawing one's attention to something.

Mosaic

Little inlaid wood tiles can produce a picture or decoration. This is called a mosaic—a way of decorating floors in a way less common than floorboards. Normally the pieces are placed four by four to make up a square. Like all other wood flooring, it comes in different sizes and thicknesses, and can be laid using various methods, including glue or screws.

Wood finishes

Wood can be colored by painting it or tinting it. It then has a smooth look, the knots and grains being hidden away. As a general rule, this type of finish does not stand up very well to scuffing feet or chair legs so it should be reserved for less stressed flooring. The best paints for woods are enamels (they give a glossy finish), semi-gloss paints, and tough paints with epoxy resins. Paints also offer the possibility of using stripped wood or decorative motifs. Parquet can be stripped and the grain of wooden furniture can be turned into a decorative element in its own right. And, of course, a skilled craftsman can use paint to create all sorts of patterns and motifs. Do not be afraid to experiment with wood: there is opportunity to give it a personal touch. However, try out your ideas on a sample first.

Staining wood is a less radical treatment than painting it. First it must be sealed with an undercoat that leaves it impermeable and ensures a consistent hue. Bleaching wood before applying the stainer will give lighter tones. When we visit a hardware store the salesperson will inform us about the three types of stains: water-based, solvent-based, and white-spirit. He or she can help us decide which one will work best for what we are doing and the wood we are working with.

DO

Choose hardwoods for spaces that have high traffic.

Use floorboards to create optical effects that will make narrow rooms seem wider, and short rooms longer.

Before installing wood, leave it in the room for a few days so it can adapt to the climatic conditions of the space it will be in.

DO NOT

Clean the parquet with a lot of water or corrosive chemical substances.

Lay down parquet in spaces over which frequently furniture is moved; it scratches easily.

Paint or stain a parquet already varnished. These treatments can only be applied to natural woods.

Hard floors

Many materials are ideal for hard, resilient, and long-lasting floors. Brick, ceramic tiles, stone slabs, and marble are all suitable options. However, before making a final decision we should weigh certain factors. Hard floors have to be installed by a professional, often working on top of a prepared foundation. This tends to make the cost of these floors higher because not only do you have to pay for material but also for workmanship.

Another consideration is that these floors are cold and hard, and they do not give under your feet. Therefore, they are not comfortable when you walk on them barefoot. Also, they do not muffle sound; instead they reflect it, often amplifying it. The final drawback is that they are too heavy for the beams of old buildings, which might not stand up to extra strain.

Despite all these factors, which could dissuade us from using these materials, they have many positive characteristics, chiefly their aesthetic properties. The colors are always natural, and often worthy of admiration. They add freshness and more ornate examples can enrich a great variety of rooms.

Brick

Tiles

Ceramic tiles

Stones

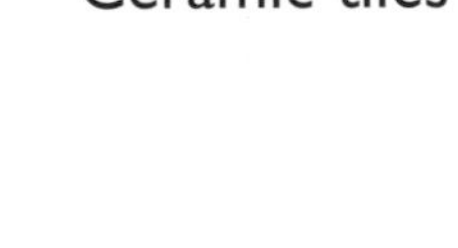

Other floors

Terrazzo

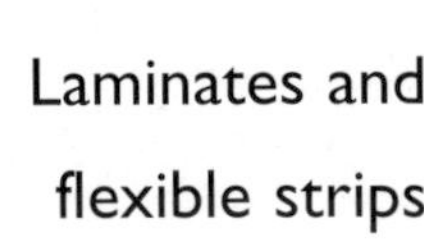

Laminates and flexible strips

Brick

Brick, along with wood and stone, is one of the most ancient construction materials. Traditionally it has been associated with houses for those who are less well off because it is cheaper than stone and marble. Brick's rustic feel makes it ideal for mountainside retreats, country homes, or farm houses. As a flooring it should be used only for ground floors as its weight can overburden upper stories.

The bricks used for floors are not the same as those used in the construction industry. Fired at a much higher

Brick gives rooms a rustic, "welcome home" feeling.

temperature, they are much more resilient. Their thickness depends on the manufacturer, the model, and where they come from. Individual countries may have their own particular style of bricks and ways of laying them, so they can be used to give a regional flavor to our home. The finishes, textures, and hues of brick all vary from region to region. Artisanal bricks, more difficult to lay, produce a cozy, rustic feel that few materials match. Another positive feature is the high resilience and durability of bricks. They are impermeable, stand up to knocks and stains, and are easy to clean. Floors are an important element in ensuring that a room feels comfortable temperature-wise. Bricks are cool in summer and hold the heat during winter. They are even more snug with under-floor heating. However, this material that offers so many advantages is not easy to install. Call in a specialist who is sure to get the mortar between the bricks right and to make the surface perfectly flat, important if the floor is to look good. While it takes time and effort, remember that a floor like this can last years so it will be worth it in the long run.

The finishes, textures, and colors of bricks are varied. When bricks from different areas and made of different materials are combined, the results are attractive.

Tiles

It is difficult to generalize when speaking about tiles because there are so many and they vary so much, especially depending on their origin. They can be vitrified, glazed, handmade, or machine made. Like bricks, being manufactured out of natural materials gives them warmth, and a texture that acquires a luster over time. However, they have a quality bricks do not offer—they can be combined in different colors. SInce they are cold and hard, they should be covered by a carpet or rug if they are placed in a bedroom. Then you can enjoy their colors and keep your feet warm.

Tiles must be installed by a professional to get an aesthetically pleasing and long-lasting result. The cost, calculated according to the square feet, runs from cheap versions to options that can be prohibitive. On top of this, we have to add the installation fee, which goes up the smaller the pieces are. Their fragility obliges us to handle them with great care—any broken or chipped ones have to be replaced. When you buy the first batch get some extra ones to have on hand in case any need to be replaced over the years. You will then be sure they match well.

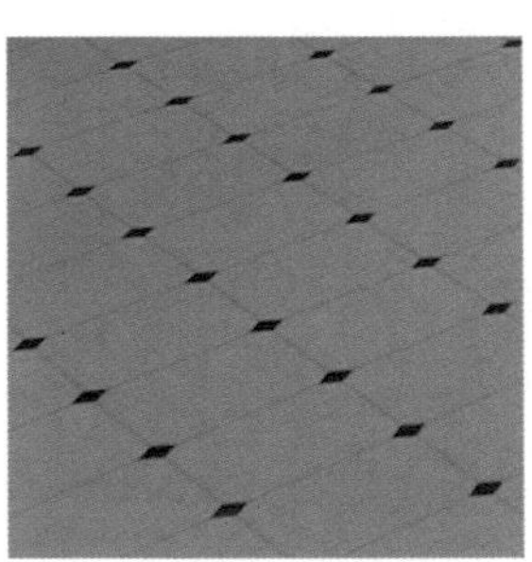

As they are easy to clean, tiles are highly suitable for spaces where there is water or food. Moreover, they offer great decorative possibilities.

Tiles are suitable for many rooms, though traditionally they have been more heavily used in bathrooms and kitchens. All the same, certain tiles are slippery when wet, so take precautions. Despite being cold on bare feet they can look beautiful and add freshness to bedrooms, entertainment areas, or living rooms. Their size must be proportional to the room. Do not tile a small bathroom with large tiles because they will lose some of their splendor. At the other extreme, small pieces in a large room tend toward boring repetition—a visual turn-off. As floor tiles must stand up to more weight than wall tiles, they are thicker. The most well-known tiles are ceramic, terracotta, and unglazed.

Ceramic tiles are manufactured from pressed refined clay. They are resilient and have a uniform color. Glazed tiles are more easily worn away. Some models are manufactured with silicon carbide used as an abrasive. There are also models with smooth finishes, engrained patterns or grooves—another way of preventing slipping. In general, clay tiles, especially glazed ones, have a clean, consistent finish and are highly suitable for modern, down-to-earth spaces. Their texture and pattern will add life and interest to the floor.

Terracotta (Italian for "baked earth") is versatile, cheap, and durable. Its finish is always a warm natural looking texture. An infinite range of tones can be obtained depending on the manufacturing process—either machine-made or, more expensive, artisanally—and the baking time. We can find restored terracotta, though it is even more costly. The fairly coarse porous nature of clay means that terra-cotta is an ideal material for country or mountainside retreats. When fired this clay assumes a color ranging from dull ochre to red. Normally it is left unglazed. It was used in the ancient world to build roof tiles. In the twentieth century there has been a revival in interest because of its aesthetic properties. However it is used, it must be made impermeable so that it is not stained by anything that may spill on it. Terracotta comes in different sizes, shapes, and thicknesses. It can be arranged into patterns or motifs. You can also design the pattern yourself, playing different tones against each other, adding character to the floor.

Unglazed tiles are manufactured from pressed baked clay, rich in silicon. They are resilient but as time goes by the lack of a glaze can become noticeable as the finish is worn away. Their color range is similar to that of terra-cotta: from natural browns to beiges and reddish hues. Nature's colors are beautiful and manufacturers use dyes to get dark tones, like sea blue. Unglazed tiles are suitable for use indoors and outdoors because when it rains they are less slippery than glazed tiles.

Encaustic tiles derive their name for the Greek word for "burning in"; this is what is done to the color. They can therefore be used for mosaics and motifs though, of course, they are more expensive. The finish is matte and consistent, but unfortunately, they tend to discolor as time goes by. Whites turn to yellow. To prevent staining they should be sealed. Throughout the twentieth century they were popular among interior designers and we will find many recovered pieces in antique shops, or even covered over with new floors in old houses. Restoring these tiled floors undoubtedly adds architectural value to a residence, and, although it may push a budget up, it should always be considered when possible.

Some tiles offer a uniform finish, fitting for rooms with crisp, modern lines.

DO

Treat terracotta to make it impermeable so it does not get stained.

Use abrasive tiles for rooms where water may be splashed, such as in the shower area.

Keep some tiles for the future so as to have a replacement supply if any become damaged.

DO NOT

Use heavy floors in old buildings: they could overload the structure.

Use inside flooring for outside. It will be slippery and it will break easily.

Use large tiles for small rooms, or tiny tiles for grand rooms.

Mosaics can be very elaborate patterns which draw attention to the floor, converting it into the star of the decoration.

Stones

Earlier, we mentioned that terracotta has a natural feeling about it, but there is nothing more natural than stone. It has been used in construction since the origins of humanity and can be found in majestic buildings such as castles and cathedrals, but also in humble homes and farms. The multitude of colors, textures, and finishes stone offers opens up many possibilities, for covering walls as well as floors. Polished stone is the most common finish, though rough textures are also possible to achieve. The thickness of the stone depends on the resilience desired.

Stone can be bought in specialized shops or in quarries. It must be laid by a specialist because of the intricacies involved. No material is exactly like stone because no two stones are the same. Stone is suitable for any type of room but once again the size must be in proportion to the room. If these simple guidelines are heeded, a stone tile floor is difficult to beat in terms of elegance.

Stones give an irregular, natural finish. We will never find two pieces exactly the same, so rooms decorated with them areunique.

Many types of stone are available on the market, each region having its own specialties. Stones can be divided into three groups according to the rocks they come from: metamorphic, sedimentary, and igneous. Metamorphic rocks were formed at high temperatures and pressures, which explains their hardness. Marble and slate are the most commonly known rocks from this group. Sedimentary rocks are formed out of sediments and organic material, they are less resilient, and their finish is textured. Sandstone and limestone, both widely used in construction, belong to this group. Finally, igneous rocks are the oldest. Their finish is the shiniest because of their crystalline properties. Granite is the most renowned igneous stone. Old stones that have already been used to build ancient buildings are sometimes recycled through the construction market. We must check where they come from to ensure that artistic or cultural treasures are not being destroyed for short-run, unethical profits.

Granite is a granular rock composed of orthoclase, albite feldspars, and quartz, usually together with other minerals, such as mica, hornblende, or augite. It is resilient, hard, impermeable, and stands up well to chemical agents. Its finish depends on the use we have in mind for it. However, as it becomes slippery when splashed by water, a rough finish is best for the kitchen or bathroom. Over time things will rub against granite, polishing it, and wearing away this roughness. Professional stonemasons can restore a stone's original qualities, but this can be costly.

Limestone comes in softer tones than granite, although we can also find darker tones that are not as vivid as crystalline granite. Limestone is cheaper than granite, though it is also less resilient. It is worn away more quickly over time, and does not stand up to chemical agents as well as granite does.

Stone can be cut to measure and then different sizes and colors can be fitted together to form the design or pattern we need.

Sandstone is halfway between granite and limestone in terms of resilience. It is also an economical option.

Marble is the best-known stone and the most highly valued due to its presence in so many buildings through the ages. Perhaps overuse and imitations are the reasons it has not been so much the rage in the twentieth century, though design is bringing it back in its purest forms. Contemporary marble is limestone in a more or less crystalline state and capable of taking a high polish. It occurs in a wide range of colors (from the purest whites, greens, blues, and pinks to black) and variations depending on where it is obtained. So what we can achieve with it is influenced by where we live. Importing it is possible but not so affordable, Italian marble being especially prized. The purity of marble refers to its imperfections and the traces of other materials it contains. It is curious that while marble without veins is the purest, it is not the most expensive. Like wrinkles on a handsome man's face, veins in marble bestow character upon it. Marble comes in fin-

Marble is widely used in bathrooms because of its elegant, understated look.

Having natural stones means that we can enjoy the use of large uncut pieces, highly suitable for generously sized rooms with modern lines.

ishes very similar to those of other stones. Do not be so captivated by its beauty that you use it indiscriminately. If overdone it can become too cold-looking.

Slate, a fine-grained rock formed by the compression of clay and shale, comes from mountainous zones. Its dark hues—grays, violets, blues, and reds—are always favored by subtle and attractive nuances. Different finishes, serrated or polished, can be achieved. It is cheaper than marble and granite, impermeable, resilient, and needs less looking after.

The list of stone floors goes on to include paving stones and pebbles, more common in the open air but producing interesting effects indoors. Artificial stones are also available; some of them created by joining together chunks of different stones to give an irregular look, or by mixing powder from crushed stones for a homogeneous finish.

Concrete is yet another possibility. It can be treated with paint or other mediums to give a finish similar to that of stone. Although there are very good reproductions available, the best policy is to steer away from these types of materials as the results are mediocre, unless we are actually aiming at a dramatic decorative effect, not trying to hide the fact that the finish is artificial.

Although the most common stone finish is polished, shiny, and consistent, a more natural finish gives it texture and a homey feel.

Just as important as the floor material is the way it is laid. You can play with the width of the seam between the pieces: they can be hardly noticeable, close together, or open, clearly visible lines.

DO

Make porous stones impermeable to avoid staining.

Make stone abrassive if placed either outside or inside when it comes into contact with water to avoid the risk of slipping on it.

DO NOT

Place stone floors in areas where you are going to walk barefoot. They are too hard and cold. Carpets or rugs can solve this problem.

Use white marble in kitchens or similar areas. This marble is porous and easily stainable. Any stain made will not disappear even when polished.

Hard floors are elegant but cold-looking. Their firmness means they are ideal for heavily used spaces such as corridors and stairs.

Stone correctly treated stands up well to dirt, becoming more attractive as time goes by.

Floorings

Terrazzo

Terrazzo is a mosaic flooring or paving composed of chips of broken stone, usually marble, and cement, polished when in place. It is widely used because of its resilience, its durability, its reasonable price, and the quality of the finish offered. The aesthetics depend on the size of the chunks used and the coloring of the material used to aggregate the mixture. Symmetrical or geometric patterns, very suitable for modern interiors, are available. It can be manufactured in the building where it is going to be used, thus ensuring a continuous finish appropriate for spaces used by many people. To draw the pattern desired, use fine metal rods, or strips, and later remove them or incorporate them as part of the scheme marking off the different colors.

Many people use terrazzo for their homes because it offers many of the advantages of marble but at a more competitive price.

Terrazzo gives a regular finish: the bigger the slabs, the more uniform the floor looks.

Ceramic tiles

A mosaic floor normally has a decorative pattern made up of small pieces of inlaid stone. An infinite range of finishes and combinations are possible due to the smallness of the pieces. However, the advantage is that elaborate patterns can be designed. The little tiles, also known as tesserae (Latin for "cubes" or "dice"), are made from marble, stone, ceramic, or terracotta, all of which can be combined. Laying them requires technical insight so call in a specialist—it will not be cheap but they are sure to produce a smooth and uniform surface that harmonizes with the rest of the decoration. As the tesserae are so small, the floor setting is very important: its finish must be classy and the color must be appropriate for the size and shape of the pieces. If it is dark it will intensify the dark colors and create a more graphic effect. A light color will compensate for intense tones. Like the majority of stone or marble floors, mosaic is generally used in kitchens and bathrooms because of its cold, hard look. Because of its cost (on the steep side) it is often combined with bigger pieces of marble or stone.

Painstaking to install, mosaic gives satisfactory results, but do not abuse its beauty because you could overload a room with detail.

Other floors

Materials such as concrete, metal, or crystal are not very common for floors and the general public is less aware of what they offer. However, they are sure winners for modern designs and the aesthetics are unbeatable. Concrete is often eschewed for being too industrial, but, in fact, it can be treated in a number of ways that render this connotation invalid. It can be painted, plastered, polished, or waxed. The finished look is sleek and meets a very important requisite for floors: resistance to wear.

Aluminum and **galvanized steel** are the metals most commonly used for floors. They come in laminated forms, normally with geometric grooves so that the floor is not slippery. In bathrooms and kitchens, aluminum is a safer bet because it does not rust. The laminates are glued or tacked to the underflooring, which can be wooden or concrete. The former is more highly recommended because of its flexibility and warmth.

Crystal sparks peoples' imagination but has never caught on because of its cost. The finish is luxuriously spectacular. The glass tiles are joined together by neoprene synthetic rubber. Thick tempered glass, adequately treated to make it non-slippery, is the best option to bear the weight and stand up to the thuds. Talk to a specialist who can advise you as to just how thick the material must be to stand up to the use you will put it through.

The brilliance of polished concrete looks good. Added to its versatility, this means that it can be used in any room.

Laminates and flexible strips

The materials we have already discussed can be used for floors in the form of laminated strips, the difference being based on the way they are laid. Laminated strips are longer, so installing them is more complicated. Whatever you do, the underfloor must be smooth, for any bumps will not be hidden by the floor surface.

These laminated floorings can be either synthetic or natural. Man-made floor coverings are usually classified as resilient floors. The most common materials are cork (natural and cheap at the same time), linoleum, and rubber. Synthetic materials, like vinyl, tend to imitate natural materials such as stone or marble but the results are generally less satisfactory. However, there are many points in their favor: their warmth, softness to touch, and easy maintenance. These things considered, we may decide to ignore an imitation's lack of realism. Imitation floor tiles are very common in stores as they offer a whole array of colors and finishes to create low cost, imaginative floors.

Laminates allow us to do our own floor design. They share two qualities with wood: they look warm and are pleasing to touch.

Laminates are simple to install but the work must be done on top of a perfectly smooth surface. Special types of glue for each material are applied. These materials are not suitable for floors subject to humidity because eventually glues will lose their hold and wrinkles will form.

Cork, which is not a synthetic, is handsome, though difficult to maintain and not particularly durable. However, its tones and finish are warm, and added to its softness and versatility, it is a great favorite for children's bedrooms. Another characteristic is that it muffles noise and maintains warmth. The downside is that it is not very resilient and is easily worn out by heavy circulation. Fun designs can be dreamed up using colored cork available in stores.

Linoleum, another natural material, has many of the advantages of synthetic products: it is strong and suitable for heavy-duty uses. It comes in many colors and designs but has suffered the negative publicity of being associated with its use in hospitals and other institutions, and is therefore not very commonly used in homes. However, its resilience means that it never disappeared completely and it is now making a comeback. One period of time when it was in fashion was at the beginning of the twentieth century when architects such as Mies van der Rohe exploited its numerous qualities, using it to produce spectacular designs. It is manufactured by coating burlap or canvas with linseed oil, powdered cork, and resin, and adding pigments to create the desired colors and patterns. This mixture of materials makes it as flexible and as insulating as cork, as hard as stone, and as warm as wood. It has one more unique advantage: it is antibacterial and, therefore, especially good for rooms that must be very hygienic. Nowadays, modern cutting techniques mean that high quality, detailed designs and patterns can be created. Being available in so many different colors makes it highly suitable for adding an original touch to our home.

Rubber shares many of the advantages of linoleum. It comes in a wide range of colors, is flexible, waterproof, resilient, warm, quiet, and has the advantage of being fire-resistant, which linoleum is not. Its industrial aesthetic led to rubber being eschewed for home decoration, but today's aesthetics have given it a new lease on life. Although rubber's origin used to be natural, nowadays synthetic forms are more common. Some of the synthetic textures imitate the finish of other floorings with grooves or wedges.

Vinyl, or PVC, is the name given to a whole range of synthetic materials fabricated by polymerization of chloride compounds with this the vinyl group. They can be manufactured with different thicknesses and sizes that enable us to cover wide spaces without seams. They share many of the advantages of the materials we have already discussed. They can be given almost any appearance, are economical and easy to maintain, and, moreover, are resistant to chemical products. They are also used to imitate wood and marble, but with better results than linoleum.

Leather is a final possibility that can be included. Its high quality and luxurious look is reflected in price. Warm, flexible, comfortable, resilient, and a good acoustic insulator, its aesthetics are similar to those of wood. It is glued down to a wooden floor and then waxed to protect it from humidity. However, it is not really suited for life in either the kitchen or the bathroom.

Textile floors

Exceptionally snug underfoot, carpets have the disadvantages of being susceptible to wear and the fact that dust gets trapped in them. However, their beauty means that they are popular in modern interiors. Naturally, they tend to be used in places with cooler climates. Natural fibers, helped by new technology, are becoming increasingly common in our carpets, adding their warmth, vivid colors and soft comfort. They can be tricky to tack down, but if well done creases will not appear. Avoid spills because stains are hard to remove from carpeting. Special treatments for grease stains are available.

Common in cold countries, carpets give the home a snug feeling.

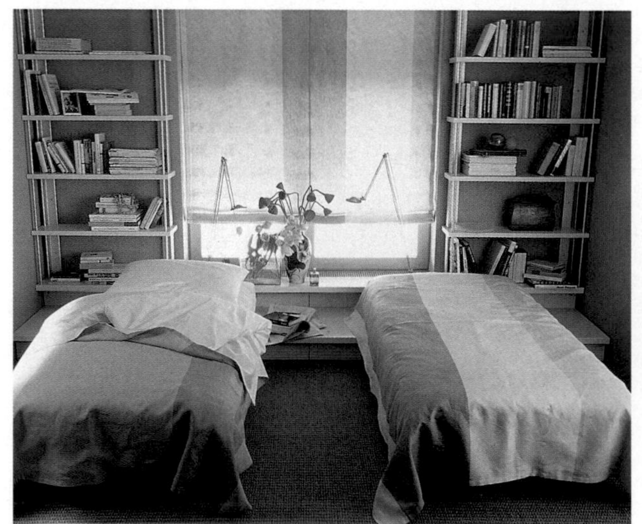

Natural fibers

Carpets and rugs

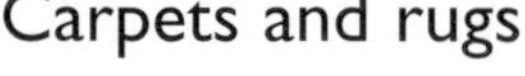

Natural fibers

Natural fiber carpets are widely used in modern interiors because of the charm of the subtle variations in their hues and shades. They are fresh, comfortable, economical, and contemporary. The most common natural fibers, are 1- agave, 2-jute (soft and not very resilient), 3-rattan, and 4-sisal (coarser).

Agave has quite a smooth finish and is clean and easy to maintain. Only found in natural colors because it cannot be dyed, it is suitable for all types of rooms provided that it is not subject to excessive humidity.

Jute comes in different tones, though with a tendency toward paleness. Its finish is soft and it is not so appropriate for heavy-duty use. Nor is it stain resistant so apply a protective solution to it before use.

Rattan fibers are coarse and very durable. One of their advantages is that they can be used in bathrooms and kitchens because the natural fibers need a little humidity to maintain their natural properties.

None of the fibers mentioned so far are as renowned as **sisal**. With a look that cannot be defined as either coarse or smooth, it is suitable for all rooms and circumstances. It is available in many different tones. It should be treated to protect against stains and dirt.

Natural fibers can also be used for wall hangings, even to cover an entire wall. We should probably leave this task to a professional because of its complexity.

Carpets give a space a natural look and feel. However, they are made of delicate materials and often do not stand up well to humidity.

Carpets and rugs

Carpets are not widely used in warm countries, but in northern Europe and the United States, they are a basic decorative feature. Carpets give a lovely sensation when you walk over them, especially barefoot, and also offer interesting aesthetic possibilities. They are seamless and therefore unify spaces, but also can be used to mark off zones, or areas of activity. They permit versatile solutions for our interior design due to the colors, textures, and finishes they come in. When choosing a carpet, bear in mind that it will be tacked down, or fitted, and can last many years if well looked after so it will have to be easily adaptable to any new decoration style we may wish to achieve. Another quality of carpets is the acoustic and thermal insulation they provide. They are suitable for all the rooms

in the house, except in the bathroom and kitchen unless you are prepared to make the extra effort to ensure they do not get wet or stained when bathing or cooking. Unfortunately, they can get dirty easily and may be difficult to clean. They are not the most hygienic of floors.

When choosing a carpet, take into consideration its texture, pile, the yarn, weight, density, color, and design. Most carpets are made of sheep's wool, which is durable, dyes readily, and handles easily. The weight of the carpet pile is directly related to its resilience (the thicker a carpet is, the more appropriate it will be for heavy-duty use). As wall hangings, light-weight carpets are better.

DO

Vacuum carpets regularly so that neither dust nor dirt accumulates in them.

Make sure all carpets used on the floor are designed for floor use; some carpets are intended for wall use.

Use special adhesives to glue the carpet to the floor, especially when subject to humidity.

DO NOT

Use carpets or rugs if you have pets or if you or your family members suffer from allergies to dust: they get dirty easily.

Put carpets or rugs near fireplaces, unless they are fire-resistant.

Place carpets or rugs in rooms that are in contact with the outdoors or where lots of people pass through.

Carpets are ideal for bedrooms because of their feet-warming qualities and their catching color designs.

Carpets combine superbly with wood and stone to give a cozy country feel.

TEN HELPFUL HINTS

1 If we want to make a space feel warmer, we must use floors that are soft on our feet, such as wood, carpets, or rugs.

2 For floors that are heavily used or in contact with the open air, use durable materials like stone, marble, tiles, and some types of hardwoods.

3 To change a room's look rapidly and economically, use fabric: as curtains, for the carpet, or to cover the furniture.

4 Give natural floors, such as terracotta or wood, adequate protection periodically to prolong their lives. They are fine materials and need special care.

5 Use curtains to filter light and to create a mood. They increase intimacy in a space.

6 For an austere or classic atmosphere, the best floor material is marble.

7 Tiles are easy to keep clean and they resist humidity.

8 If a space seems cold or bleak, it can be warmed up by curtains and carpets, or by furniture upholstery.

9 The materials chosen for floors and wall coverings must fit in with the style of a whole house.

10 To give a country feel to a room, use natural floors like stone or wood.

WALL COVERINGS

paint • wallpaper • fabric wall converings • natural fibers

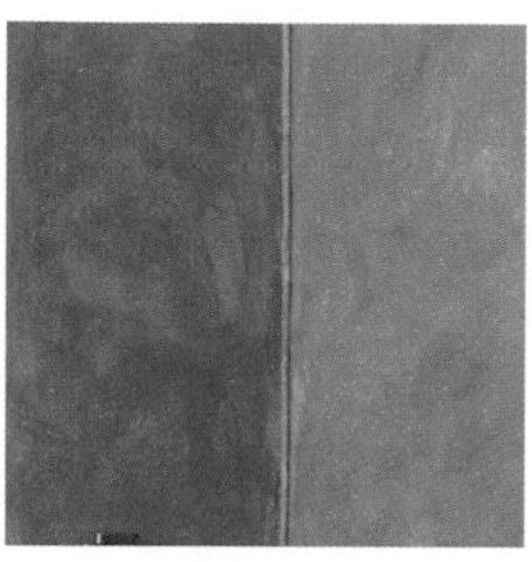

tiles • stuccowork • wood • other materials

Wall coverings

When we are decorating a room and adapting it to our needs, we must never lose sight of the walls' importance. They occupy a great deal of area and also serve to divide space. They must be carefully considered when you are working out the need for privacy and the lighting effects. Walls are visually significant because of their large surface area. In addition, their placement and their aesthetic treatment can alter a person's perception of space. The ceiling must not be left out of the equation either, for it too has a great visual impact.

Colors also modify our perception of space. Warm, dark tones make a room seem smaller and cozier. Light, cool colors make a room appear more spacious, as if the walls are receded. Color is the first variable, followed by texture and design, all of which must be considered when approaching the wall decoration.

If we pay attention to these factors we will be able to get the most out of the walls in a home and give personality to the rooms we are decorating.

Materials

Besides their role in the decoration scheme, walls also have heat retention and acoustic functions. They offer the inhabitants of the home intimacy. For these reasons they must be correctly maintained and be free from dampness. However, if they do suffer from humidity, we must call in a specialist to resolve the problem before it gets worse. Warm, heat retaining materials, such as plaster and wood, are best for keeping heat in. If our primary concern is to muffle noise, we can use textured coverings like stone or fabric.

Ceilings require different treatment; depending in part on how high they are, the finish, and the other elements in the room. A high ceiling should be dark and textured so that it is seems lower. If there is some furniture we want to have stand out in the room, we can paint the ceiling a light color to turn it into a background. If, alternatively, the ceiling is interesting in its own right because of moldings or plaster work, painting it white will suffice, though we can consider doing the cornices a different color. This depends on what the space is like and if it already has enough points of interest. However, whatever we do we must always consider the total scheme. No wall or ceiling in itself should be designed or selected without regard for it. If the room being decorated is full of shapes that do not follow any one pattern, we can use the walls and ceiling to unify them.

Remember that the total scheme is more important than the individuality of any one feature. The materials chosen must be compatible with the overarching scheme.

CADBURY'S

Paint

Painting is the most economical way of bringing the walls to life, and the one that gives the most surprising results. Its effects can be seen immediately, so we can modify the plan as we go along. Professionals can tell us which of the extensive range fo paints will best suit our needs. We must not only consider the finish (gloss, satin, or matte) that we are seeking, we also have to take into consideration the surface being treated. Will it have to withstand humidity? Must it be washable? All these factors will influence our decision.

Enamel paints are water-based, have good covering power, and dry quickly, though they tend to be less long-lasting. Lacquers reflect a lot of light and give energy to a room. There are various types of solvent-based paints: gloss, semi-gloss, and enamels. Enamels are washable and are ideal for applying to wood and metal. Solvent-based paints should be used on perfect surfaces, because they

Paint is inexpensive, easy to apply, and very effective.

DO

Use paint and wallpaper when you want to change the look of a room but do not have a lot of time (or money). These changes are easy to undo or modify later on.

Make sure that the paint or wallpaper is water-resistant.

DO NOT

Use unwashable paint or wallpaper in spaces likely to get dirty, such as children's bedrooms.

Paint on top of wallpaper. Either the paint will not stick properly, or both the paint and the wallpaper will peel off.

exaggerate imperfections. If the wall to be painted is in any way 'rough', the best thing to do is to use matte or satin paints which help to hide these imperfections. Temperate paints are more natural and therefore their colors are warmer (although modern technology does offer us excellent artificial colors). Certain paints provide us with the opportunity to create special effects. One such paint is made of a mixture of white spirit and varnish in a ratio of two to one, added to solvent-based paint. The result is a glossy, elegant, and luminous paint. Water-based paint can be diluted until it allows the color underneath to peek through.

Paint goes on well even in bathrooms. Splashes present no problems for water-resistant paints.

EDITORS
04

Wallpaper

We have already seen how paints offer many possibilities and can quickly give a new look to a room. The same can be said of wallpaper. Stores stock all sorts of wallpaper patterns, ranging from flowers, stars, and stripes, to geometric shapes and pictures for children. We are sure to find something that fits in with what we are seeking. To make the decoration even more varied, we can combine paint with wallpaper. The choice of paper will be influenced by what type of atmosphere we wish to create. However, the old rule about size and pattern still applies: in general, big patterns only look good in large rooms, and small ones in small rooms.

The wall must be prepared before the wallpaper is put up. Scrape off the old paint or wallpaper until you are down to the original wall. Apply a primer undercoat to seal the surface, then paste the back of the paper. Let it stand for five minutes to bond and then stick it to the wall, taking care to the lines straight. The paste mixture can also be applied to the wall, but this is optional. Ensure that the pattern is correctly lined up between the different strips. Finally, use a brush to take out any air bubbles or creases.

With so many different types of paper available, there is sure to be one that meets our needs.

If the upholstery, wallpaper, and curtains all match up well, the total scheme will be very effective.

LYING IN BED

Wallpaper can be manufactured in two ways: with a molded pattern or with machine-printed patterns. The former are more expensive but stand up better to the passing of time (the colors are practically inalterable). The latter are more economical (some can be wiped clean) and they are more resistant to tearing due to their vinyl content. White wallpaper is also on the market: you paint it once it is on the wall, using silhouette shapes and creating your own pattern (if you want to give the children an opportunity to have some clean fun).

DO

Make sure that the wallpaper color and pattern matches the total scheme.

Protect the wallpaper with a baseboard.

Buy extra paper to ensure you can repair any stain or tear in the future.

DO NOT

Use big patterns in small rooms, or small, repetitive patterns in large rooms.

Place wallpaper up to the ceiling in small or narrow rooms. Instead, use wallpaper up to halfway up the wall and then finish off the decoration with paintwork. It will make the room seem more spacious.

Put up the wallpaper without first having prepared the wall. Both the paint and the wallpaper would exaggerate the imperfections.

Wallpaper makes it easy to give a period feel to a room.

Fabric wall coverings

Fabrics give results quite similar to those of wallpaper. They too come in patterns and are especially suitable for homes in which we wish to muffle the sound. Decorating with fabric is a little more complicated than using paper, unless the wall is perfectly smooth (the procedure is then very similar to wallpaper). If there are any bumps or ridges in the wall the task is trickier but at least we do not have to repair the entire wall.

Any type of fabric can be used, though the best are thicker, not excessively elastic ones (they are easier to paste up). The most common way of fixing the fabric to the wall is by stapling it to some panels. The staples are then

Fabric wall coverings are classy and cozy. Be very careful not to tear or stain them.

hidden away behind a trim. It must be carefully placed to ensure there are no creases and that the pattern is correctly lined up. Padding can be placed between the fabric and the wall to increase the acoustic muffling characteristics and to make the room cozier.

Fabrics offer a wide range of decorative possibilities.

DO

Use fabrics, especially with padding, to deaden the sound in a home.

Make sure that the colors and patterns of the wall fabrics, bedlinen, and tablecloths all team up well together.

Use trims and friezes to give a high-quality finish to fabric coverings.

DO NOT

Place fabrics in rooms where they can easily get dirty, such as the kitchen or children's bedrooms.

Slip into bad taste by overusing loud patterns or incompatible pattern combinations.

Natural fibers

Natural fibers include materials as varied as raffia, cork, and hessian, all of which have a natural origin. Stores sell them prepared on a paper or fabric support to give them some rigidity, ready to be fitted. Pay attention to the seams when using these materials, covering them up with trims, strips, or even including them as part of the design.

SA
NTA
L

Tiles

So varied are the wall tiles sold in shops that a whole world of possibilities is opened up. Like floor tiles, different versions are available. Wall tiles are thinner and lighter than floor tiles and installing them demands even more attention as they are more visible. They have always been a traditional feature in bathrooms and kitchens because of their resistance to water and the ease with which they are cleaned; these qualities also work well sometimes in other rooms. Few coverings are as durable. Nevertheless, use tiles with moderation because in excess they make a room too cold and impersonal; it is a good idea to combine them with other materials like stuccowork and paint.

Tiles are especially suitable for bathrooms and kitchens because they stand up well to the humidity and constant cleaning.

All the different tile finishes open up a world of possibilities for functional spaces like the bathroom and the kitchen; functionality does not have to be boring.

Stuccowork

Stuccowork used to be quite popular but the emergence of cheaper, more modern techniques—which did not require professional assistance—pushed aside traditional decoration techniques. The preference for old-style or artisanal decoration has enabled stuccowork to make a comeback. Stucco-like finishes of acceptable quality have also appeared, the majority based on paint. The advantage of stuccowork, however, is that when done well it produces a shiny, resilient, uncompromising quality finish not easily matched by other techniques. Not surprisingly, the cost is high. Chemical advances mean that today products which look similar to stuccowork, and are as long-lasting, are available. Whether you opt for the real thing or an imitation will depend on your budget.

DO

Use stuccowork for spaces where people pass back and forth, and even for bathrooms. Stuccowork is ideal because it is very durable and also washable.

Use tiles, easy to clean and impermeable, for bathrooms and kitchens.

DO NOT

Put porous tiles made of materials such as terra-cotta in bathrooms or kitchens without first making them water resistant.

Use small tiles to cover large walls, or big tiles for small spaces.

Wood

Wall paneling has been popular for hundreds of years because a natural wood texture adds warmth and elegance to a room, and also acts as acoustic insulation. The advantage of wood is that it is strong, stiff, relatively light, and flexible. Wood paneling is installed in a way similar to wood floors (on top of frames—stiles and rails—which in turn grip the wall) and so can be used to give a smooth finish to damaged walls. To do this, however, call in a specialist to ensure that the panels are evenly placed.

Wood wall coverings require the same care and attention as wood floors. Wood is a natural, renewable resource, and so we must be sure only to use supplies from sustainable forests. Besides buying new wood, we can also explore the idea of recovering panels from old houses and from antique dealers. With a little imagination, even old doors and windows can be put to good use covering the walls.

Although traditionally wood has been eschewed in the bathroom, contemporary designers are including it because once it has been given an adequate anti-humidity treatment it can stand up to heavy use.

Other materials

Wall coverings offer us as many possibilities as floors. So many materials around us can enrich the decoration of our homes if we apply some imagination. Not many people consider metal, but in tile or laminate form it can give a modern air to a room. Glass panes can replace a dim wall and add luminosity as they visually connect different spaces in the home. Often glass and metal will be too cold for bedrooms, but they enhance the atmosphere in less personal spaces, such as the foyer, hallways, and even the bathroom. Leather, an extremely warm material, is difficult to beat in terms of style and lavishness.

Apart from these natural materials, modern technology offers the advantage, of good aesthetics and practicality. A good example are plaster panels that require no water for their installation. No plaster or cement need be added either. The panels are first mounted on a metal frame to make them rigid; then they are painted or prepared over, according to your tastes. These systems have many advantages, the most obvious being the ease with which they are installed and later kept clean. Different types of panels are available for different acoustic, humidity, and heat conditions.

Wall coverings offer many possibilities. Concrete, a cold, industrial looking material, is good for more modern spaces.

Restored stone in old buildings is highly decorative and attractive.

Another possibility to explore is that of old, valuable materials hidden away beneath a layer of plaster or wallpaper. We can do a little test around the house, or on the wall in question. If we do find anything of interest, and it is economically worthwhile to preserve it, we can strip away all the paper or plaster. Recovering an old wall covering, whether it be tiles or even attractive brickwork, will make the house more charismatic—something we can all appreciate.

Glass bricks, popular in the seventies, have come back into fashion. They let through bits of light without taking away intimacy.

DO

Before installing a new covering in old houses, be sure that valuable decorative material is not hidden away beneath paint or paper.

Be bold enough to use concrete or metal in modern, non-nitimate rooms in the home (not in bedrooms). These materials give more character to the decoration.

DO NOT

Use wood for wall coverings on ground floors because it may be adversely affected by the humidity.

Use heavy materials to cover walls of old buildings; they may overload the structure.

1. The ceramic floor gives the room a "country" feel.

2. The white cabinets and countertop, combined with the stainless steel, creates a sense of cleanliness in the kitchen.

3. The terracotta tone feels comfortably casual and contrasts beautifully with the white furnishings.

4. A rug marks off the dining area and makes the floor more comfortable underfoot.

5. Easy-to-clean marble protects the walls from dirt and grease.

Many of the materials that surround us can be used as coverings. Our imagination will define the limits.

THE TEN MOST HELPFUL TIPS

1 If you want to change a room's look but do not have a lot of time, wall-paper, paint and fabrics are the safest way.

2 The colors of the walls allow you to define the function of spaces within a global area.

3 Stuccowork is resilient and impermeable. It is ideal for rooms constantly passed through or that get dirty easily. Being practical has taken nothing away from its aesthetics, either.

4 Tiles are perfect for bathrooms and kitchens. Almost anything is possible, in terms of creativity, due to the wide variety of models and finishes.

5 Dare to use wood in rooms were originally it was rejected, such as the kitchen and bathroom. Treat it correctly to protect it from the humidity.

6 Marble is optimal for creating a classic, classy atmosphere. However, it is also very much "in" for pure contemporary, cutting edge interiors.

7 Natural fibers can be used for coverings; they are especially suitable for improving the acoustics of a room.

8 Metal or concrete panels are old materials applied with new techniques yet to be fully exploited. Dare to try them out in corridors, halls and landings.

9 Staircases are ideal spaces for trying out new ideas with glass and metal.

10 When choosing wall coverings make sure that they fit in with the total scheme, with the flooring and the furniture. The cohesion of the whole project comes before individual elements.

Color

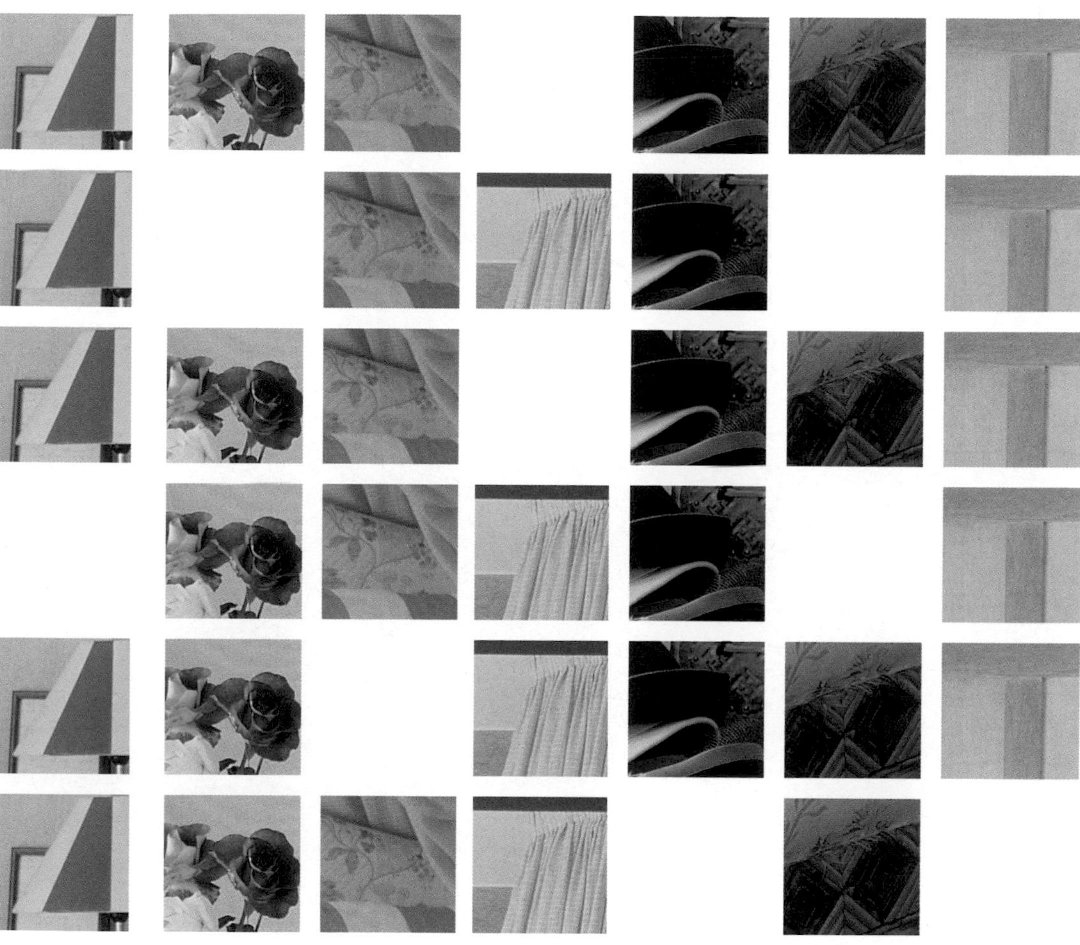

"Color is a way of directly influencing the soul.
Color is the key. The eye, the hammer.
The soul is the piano with many strings."

Wassily Kandinsky

INTRODUCTION

harmony and contrast • defining a color

Introduction

Color is one of the most powerful tools in decoration. The dominant tone in a room will define the character and mood of the space. If we want to get the mood right, we must be attuned to color's possibilities, its psychological effects, and the best ways of combining color palettes.

It is said that each artist has his or her own palette; the same is true for every one of us. As we move through life our personal evolution is reflected in the way we dress, the objects we acquire, and how we decorate (or would like to decorate) where we live. By following some basic rules, we can make our palette more disciplined and coherent, and get as much as possible out of our color scheme.

Decoration has to serve three purposes: it must make a room feel comfortable; it has to be practical; it must allow for easy interaction with other people, such as family and those who visit us.

Art and nature are the two most important sources of inspiration for decoration. The surest way of getting the color composition right is to decorate a space using a painting or a landscape that reflects our tastes in color as a guide. In a painting, analyze the importance and quantity of each color. What proportion of the canvas does it cover? Try to see how the colors are spread out and how they interact. This composition can then be reproduced in the decoration, using the same proportions.

Color can make a room stimulating, balanced, soothing, or practical. Organize the colors so that each room has the right feel for the activity going on there. In an office we will create a stimulating atmosphere, in the living room a more relaxing one. Every color has its own personality, and whether we are warm, cold, intimate, or easy-going, we will find a palette of colors that fits the way we are and how we want to feel.

Color has the power to mark off areas and to define functions, and it is used in this way not only at home. Highly effective, color coordination is used in industry and public places. The same principle applies to our home. Color can tell us where a space designated for one purpose begins and ends without having to use physical barriers. Color also has the capacity to make a space seem ordered, or to create sub-areas within a larger space. In contrast, it can also unify a space, though this does not

mean that all one room should be the same (monotonous) color. Whatever we are using color for, never break away from the general color scheme. We must combine textures and understated tone variations to make the furnishings of a space blend together. Color has to work within a room, but it can also serve as the link between two spaces. In one room one particular color may only be a little dash, a detail, while in the next room it may be the theme color, as perhaps a third color leads us into another room. Color schemes can also draw together rooms; in these cases it must be sufficiently compelling to hold the attention and organize the space. The best rule of thumb is to stay within one color range (either the warm colors or the cold ones), using the tones that bring out the best in the room. In small rooms we can play with visual links so that our eyes roam and feel that there is something more to the space than is immediately apparent. For spaces that seem too big and empty, repeating a pattern gives us the feeling that a room is smaller and not so foreboding.

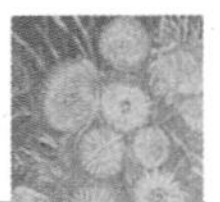

Harmony and contrast

To use color effectively we must bear in mind some basic principles. Colors and shades are so varied that they must be organized into schemes; otherwise we would not be able to work efficiently with them. Rules about color are not to be applied absolutely, however. In the world of color there are no immovable limitations; everything, including the color combinations, is a question of personal taste.

There are two types of color schemes: harmonies and contrasts. First we will deal with harmonious schemes.

• **Monochromatic schemes.** A monochromatic scheme uses shades and hues of only one color. Such a limited palette means we run the risk of designing a boring space, but if we get it right, we can create a harmonious space. The difference is often subjective.

• **Analogous colors.** These colors are next to each other on the color wheel; they shares tones and shades. Reddish purple, purple, and bluish purple are similar: they all have purple in common. Analogous colors combine together. For example a violet cushion goes well with a blue sofa.

A monochromatic color scheme makes a room harmonious and coherent. In this room a dash of color provides a contrast.

Color contrasting schemes are based on complementary colors and pairs of colors that are opposite each other on the color wheel. For example, red is the complement of green, and blue is the complement of orange. When two complementary colors are placed side by side, it seems as if they vibrate; this energizing contrast stands out.

• **Three colors (triads).**
Color schemes can be made up of three colors distributed evenly around the color wheel. They can be primary colors (such as yellow, magenta, and cyan). An intense version of this combination can be uncomfortable for the spectator (example: an Andy Warhol picture). Or we can try secondary colors (green, orange, and purple), which combined are not so provocative.

• **Four colors (tetrads).**
These color schemes are made up of two pairs of complementary colors, for example, orange and blue next to a greenish yellow and violet.

• **Divided complementary colors.**
This scheme places a color next to the two tones on either side of its complementary color. The effect of this combination is similar to complementary colors working together but a greater number of possibilities are opened up.

• **Cold and warm colors.**
Cold and warm colors are two ranges of similar colors. Green, blue, and purple are cold colors; red orange, and yellow are warm colors.

Warm color schemes: the warm colors create a homey, sunny feel. Walls appear nearer.

Cold color schemes: the cold colors create a cold atmosphere and make walls seem further away.

Two decorative schemes based on color: playing with different tones of the same color unifies the room on the right. The contrast between primary colors—red and yellow—highlights the architectural features.

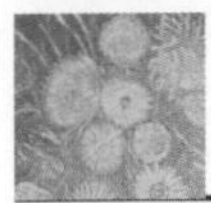

Defining a color

Three parameters define a color: hue, brightness, and saturation. Each one of these parameters deals with different aspects of the chromatic effect and enable us to make the right decision when choosing and combining colors.

The **hue** is the color itself. Yellow is one hue, green another, and blue another. Color, or the hue, is a characteristic of the surface of an object; its capacity to reflect light is what makes it one color or another.

Color does not exist without **light**. When you turn off the lights there are no colors, only black, the absence of color. Color not only varies due to the light conditions but is also influenced by the colors beside it. Light hits an object and is then reflected into the retina, the light sensitive layer behind the pupil. The image is interpreted and sent to the brain, so the color perceived depends on the amount of reflected light.

Brightness is the sensation that an object appears lighter or darker than another. The retina is sensitive to the different light waves it receives and perceives luminosity and darkness. For example, yellow is brighter than blue or green.

When decorating a home, play creatively with color. This can result in an original, upbeat feel.

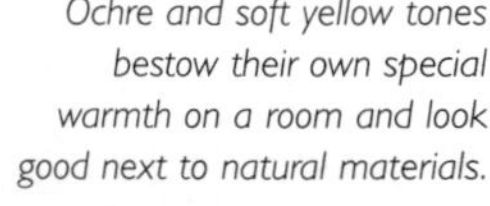

Ochre and soft yellow tones bestow their own special warmth on a room and look good next to natural materials.

Saturation refers to the degree of chroma or purity of a color. It depends directly on the amount of pure color a surface contains. Intense red, for example, is purer than pink because the latter contains white, and purer than grayish red, which is "contaminated" by black.

Yellow looks unpretentious and neat; it unifies contrasting spaces and brightens them up.

TEN HELPFUL HINTS

1 The color scheme of a room must be compatible with its size, shape, and orientation.

2 Warm colors tend to create a comfortable, intimate atmosphere. Cold colors give a sensation of greater space and elegance.

3 Use warm colors in cold rooms, and cold colors in warm rooms.

4 Emphasize the general color scheme by placing a few contrasting details.

5 Decorate large rooms with intense, dark colors and patterns.

6 Small rooms need light, cold colors to make them feel more spacious.

7 Vivid, warm contrasting colors make for stimulating, dynamic atmospheres.

8 Pale, subtle or neutral colors make for soothing rooms.

9 Neutral colors are ideal for joining together pure colors and for toning down strong ones.

10 A balanced color palette rounds out the total decoration scheme.

Combining different tones of white gives us a delicate, elegant atmosphere of timeless beauty.

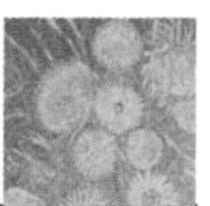

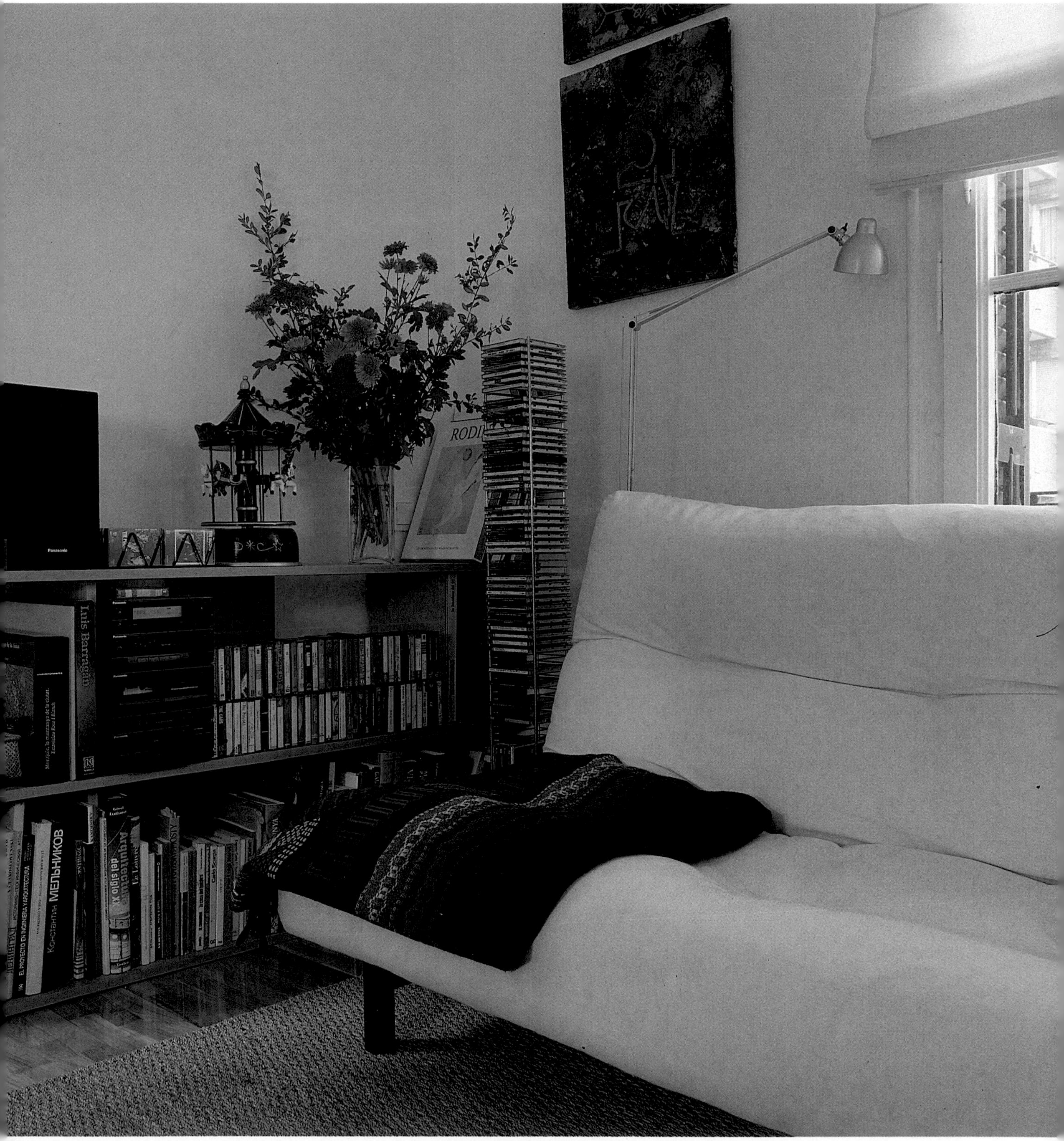
RODI
Luis Barragán
МЕЛЬНИКОВ

COLORS

whites • yellows • reds

blues • greens • blacks

Colors

When we are working on a space, remodeling it to suit our needs, we must not forget how important the walls are in the composition. They offer a lot of surface area and in addition to their aesthetic possibilities, they have three important practical functions. They directly influence our intimacy, control the sound quality, and affect the light intensity in the room.

The colors of the walls visually affects the room and how we perceive the space, an influence also exercised by the ceiling, which must be treated as part of the same equation.

Warm colors make a room seem smaller and more homey, a place where we can retreat to unwind. Light, cold colors make a room seem more spacious; they can even create the sensation that the walls recede. Color is the first variable we can play with when decorating the walls; the others are design and texture, which some interior designers have defined as the new color. For example, we may want to go for a limited color palette, but with different textures everywhere, or vice versa. There are many techniques for increasing the expressiveness of the walls and for making our home a place where we feel at ease.

White and neutral colors

White, always associated with purity, is one of the most widely used colors in decoration because it combines with all tones. Neutral colors are defined as those that contain a great deal of white but do not tend towards any of the primary or secondary colors. By this definition, pastel colors, such as pale pink or sky blue, are not neutral. Cream is considered a neutral tone. We could define neutral colors as all the achromatic tones (literally "free from color"), but this is not strictly true because beige is defined as neutral when, in fact, it belongs to the family of browns. The same holds for light grays, which come from black.

Many neutral tones are associated with natural materials—stone, earth, wood, straw, sand—or with artificial materials such as metal, glass, and concrete.

White is the ideal color for spaces with old architectural elements, or for reconciling distinct architectural styles.

CODE

Pando

Neutral tones are especially practical in the world of decoration because their neutrality means they can easily be teamed up with other colors, apart from having the quality of growing old without losing their beauty. They are calm, soothing colors and are an ideal background for hanging pictures and tapestries. If a space is overloaded, you can lighten it up with neutral tones. Contrasting decorative styles—for example, old architecture and modern furniture—can be reconciled by neutral colors. Any door, furniture, or fitting that we want to go unnoticed should be painted in neutral tones so that it does not stand out.

Many rich textures are neutral colors: sanded wood furniture, natural artist's linen, ribbon weave fabric, frame linen, wenge wood, upholstery scrim, silks, tulle, and so on.
White in tempera paint or limestone has a special tex-

Painting walls and furniture in neutral tones allows them to slip unobtrusively into the background, providing a harmonious setting for other colors and decorative details.

Colors

ture that is not equaled by modern plastic paints. If we use these traditional paints it will be easy to create a straightforward country style.

White conveys serenity and tranquility; it makes spaces appear bigger and brighter and is therefore specially suitable for small interiors or bedrooms. Pure white, when bathed in natural light, is a warm color. Under artificial light it can seem cold, a disadvantage easily overcome by adding a little red, yellow, or brown pigment. The paint will not lose the qualities of white, but it will become warmer.

A serene white space must be decorated with neutral tone objects and natural textures like wood and stone. We can add a few dramatic touches to create elegant contrasts.

DO

Take advantage of neutral tones to combine complicated colors.

Liven up rooms full of neutral tones by introducing a touch of color.

Paint small, interior bedrooms with neutral colors so that they feel bigger, warmer, and brighter.

DO NOT

Paint the objects we wish to stand out in neutral tones. This would push them into the background.

Do not use neutral bluish or grayish tones in cold spaces; red and yellow neutral tones, however, do add warmth.

Use neutral warm colors in small spaces. Grayish or bluish tones make the room seem bigger.

Neutral tones are commonly used as backdrops for restored furniture or old architecture. The furniture or the architectural element then becomes the protagonist.

White symbolizes purity, innocence, cleanliness, serenity, and peace.

We can find it almost anywhere in nature.

TEN HELPFUL HINTS

1 White and neutral tones are an ideal backdrop to make a work of art or tapestry stand out.

2 Neutral tones should be applied when a space is overloaded architecturally, or when we want something to fade into the background.

3 Neutral tones age well so they can be used where we do not redecorate, or touch up, very often; or if our intention is to specifically create an aged effect.

4 Variations on neutral tones are ideal for small rooms.

5 White and neutral tones are a great way of combining different decorative styles as they act as a neutral transition zone between one style and the other.

6 Gray metal or gray concrete, two neutral tones, are especially apt for creating modern ambiences with a cutting edge feel.

7 Textured neutral tones, like limestone or temperate paint, are perfect for creating rustic effects.

8 Neutral tone fabrics (carpets, curtains, or tapestries) are a great help when decorating because they go well with all the colors.

9 If we want a room steeped in neutral tones to be more lively, we can introduce a few dramatic color touches; dark colors, even black, are a good solution.

10 A neutral tone is perfect for painting a wall or doors that we want to be unobtrusive.

Some natural materials, such as marble and stone, enhance a room's elegance and feel good due to their neutral tones.

Yellows

Yellow, the color of the sun, has traditionally been used to paint the kitchen. Having seen the light, however, people have realized that yellow's warmth and cheerfulness are suitable for all the other rooms. It is not an exaggeration to say that yellow, like early morning sunbeams, can raise our spirits. If yellow makes you feel good in your bedroom, you can carry that mood all through the house. The great impressionist painter Monet had his dining room decorated in yellow tones: it was an exceptionally warm room. We need not go as far as he does, but we can see that yellow, whether from paintwork, wallpaper, or incandescent lighting creates a glowing, homey ambience. Associated with the sun and summer, it is widely used in tropical and Mediterranean countries, above all along the coast, where people enjoy long days in the open air.

Yellow must be handled carefully because it is so eye-catching (any poor usage will show up glaringly). Its popular use in shopping malls and on billboards has made it harder to be accepted in home decoration. Because it is an eye turner, do not overuse it; a little is sufficient generate its warmth. Yellow mixed with white produces a cream color, or a very pale yellow, that adds that little bit of warmth that white alone cannot achieve. Yellow is not

The family of yellow

always warm; a tinge of red gives it this quality. A pure, citrus yellow is tepid.

Having praised yellow so much, it is fair to point out that in some moments of history yellow has suffered negative-press: it was said to bring bad luck to actors when they performed on stage. Even worse, it was identified as the color of madness. But the history of art also has an ambassador for yellow: the Dutch painter Vincent Van Gogh made us marvel at its beauty in all its many tones in his paintings of sunflowers and cornfields. Having seen his works or just walked through the Provence fields oneself, there can be no doubt as to yellow's warmth and expressivity.

Yellow and white are easy to combine. White makes yellow's warmth stand out, while its calmness is a foil to yellow's vitality.

SALT

HISTOLOGIA FUNCIONAL
ARRECIFES DE CORAL
GUINNESS 1989
DINOSAURIOS

DO

Paint yellow next to white so that its warmth is more noticeable.

Combine it with greens, blues, and vivid pinks.

Use it in dark, cold rooms to give a homely feeling and to reinforce the natural light.

Yellow emits warm energy. It is ideal for making a bedroom or a bathroom feel cozy.

DO NOT

Combine yellow with pastel tones as the latter will look sad next to yellow.

Use an intense yellow; it does not look good when it stands out too much, and, moreover, it would need an equally energetic complementary color.

Go too far with golden yellow tones. When used moderately they warm up the ambience, but when used too much they can make a room seem pretentious and cold.

Yellow is a primary color.
We can define it as the most luminous color in the spectrum.
It is used to give warmth and to stimulate positive energy.
Its complementary color is violet.
It symbolizes warmth, energy, and happiness.
We can find it in nature: sunflowers, daffodils, primroses, the sun, and gold are all yellow.

The family of yellows

We can categorize the yellows used in decoration into four groups.

Citrus yellows are characterized by luminosity. They create a happy, youthful atmosphere. Some of these intense variations make us look twice. Avoid extremely citrus tones: they can appear to be too acidic.

Ochres and crude yellows are also luminous but quieter. They make for a warm, clean, disciplined atmosphere, although less cheerful and energetic. They hint at sumptuousness. These yellows are quite common in nature and give a home an open-air feel.

Egg yolk yellows have red in their composition and therefore even more energy and warmth. Because they are vivid tones that turn heads they are difficult to use in large quantities, but they work well as little accents or for dramatic details combined with wallpaper and patterns. They must be complemented by equally vigorous colors. Orange, with its high red content, gives rooms a tropical feel.

Gold, copper, and brass yellows are warm, elegant, classy, and even luxurious. They should be used sparingly because if you go too far you will destroy the cozy feeling.

Yellow tones combine especially well with natural colors, like wood.

In bedrooms yellow offers a homey, cozy atmosphere, giving and gives energy.

Yellow is easy to combine. Its warmth makes it appropriate for all the rooms in the house.

TEN HELPFUL HINTS

1 Yellow has positive connotations because it is associated with the sun and warm climates.

2 Because it is a warm color, yellow objects or walls appear closer.

3 Its warmth and its association with natural light make it ideal for dark, cold rooms.

4 Pale yellow is very versatile and combines well with gray, cold blue, and lavender. It evokes happiness.

5 Yellow is the ideal color for making an impersonal hallway seem a little more cozy.

6 Yellow and violet produce a vibrating contrast suitable for rooms in which there is a lot of activity.

7 Intense yellow is very warm, but it must be combined with equally intense and energetic tones so that it doesn't overload the space.

8 White tones emphasize the warmth of yellow tones.

9 Yellow is upbeat when it is next to gray, cold blue, or lavender tones.

10 Golden and copper yellow tones are perfect for creating elegant, classy rooms.

Reds

When we think about red, many things come to mind. It is the color of passion, of fire, and of blood. Historically it has warned of danger and is used in advertising to catch people's attention. It is a dominating, provocative color that reminds us of movement.

Due to its psychological effects, red is used to decorate the living room and the dining room more than other rooms. Studies into the effects of the different colors on humans have shown that red stimulates our appetite and makes us more talkative and sociable. When it is used in great quantities it provokes adrenaline flows, accelerates the heart rate, and makes us feel warmer. Although nature offers us many examples of reddish hues—sunset or terra-cotta—it is difficult to find pure examples of abundant red. In nature, rather than appearing in big blotches of color, red is more common in subtle brushstrokes and dashes that brighten up the view, such as the speckle of poppies in a green meadow. In the world of art there are numerous

Red is a bold, energetic color. It is the best way of introducing a contrasting element or a dash of color into a monotonous room.

ELLE

artists who have been attracted by the energy of pure red. Painters that stand out include Mondrian, Calder, Miró, and Lichtenstein, all of whom combined basic colors with white and black.

Such vigor and intensity means that red must be used cautiously. Large surface areas of this color are not advisable. Just as mother nature has shown us by using red sparingly, but effectively, a little dash enhances a perfectly balanced landscape. Maybe this is why red is more appropriate for city houses than for country retreats, where neutral tones, or greens and blues, dominate. Burgundy and vermilion, two variations of red, produce a glamour suitable for classic, formal atmospheres. Pure red is good for playing off against other colors and for contrasts. If red is energetic, crimson is even more so. Anything more than a little detail would be too intense. Use it sparingly to give a dramatic touch to the total scheme, but stick to more subtle tones if you do not want to make the room overwhelming.

If we look around us we can see that nature offers us natural reddish materials that can be incorporated into our home decoration. Red terracotta or wood with a reddish hue are subtle tones that provide warmth and energy without upsetting the composition. Ceramic floor, wall tiles, or soft-toned knick-knacks can all be used to add a touch of red. Bright scarlet is ideal for decorating cozy rooms like the dining room or the living room. And all these shades of red are especially gorgeous when illuminated by candlelight.

321

Red is a primary color (as magenta).
We can define it as the most energetic color in the spectrum.
It is known to accelerate the heart rate and to improve blood circulation.
Its complementary color is green.
It symbolizes passion, rage, energy, and warmth.
We can find it in nature in rubies, roses, poppies, and clay.

DO

Use pink to decorate spaces used mainly at night. When lit by candles or soft lighting the ambience is warm and homey.

Use pink in small, dark spaces to brighten them up and make them feel bigger.

Use natural reds, the color of the earth and terracotta, to decorate spaces we want to feel naturally warm.

DO NOT

Use the colder pink tones (they contain blue in their composition) in cold, dark atmospheres.

Use feminine pinks (they have been overused in decorating little girls' bedrooms).

Use shades of dark red when decorating dimly lit rooms. Although they provide warmth, they will make the room feel darker.

The family of reds

Pure red is the brightest and most brilliant tone. It reminds us of movement, passion, and warmth. Do not overuse. Its intensity requires combined with equally intense tones. Too much color ends up dazzling us. There are psychological effects to be considered. One should not be so stimulated at home.

Burgundy and vermilion are less brilliant but just as intense. They add elegance, opulence, and sumptuousness to the rooms they grace. Their earthy tones give a cool, autumn-in-the-country feel. Their warmth is a perfect complement for blues, greens, whites, and even golden shades.

Pink shades have to be dealt with separately from reddish hues. Pink is a friendly, luxurious, pleasant color that warms up a room and gives it energy but does not catch the eye in quite the same way as red. Pay attention to which pink tones you choose; it is best to avoid the typical feminine ones used for little girls' bedrooms. Pinks combine well with white and shades of blue and contrast harmoniously with yellows.

Red makes a space more elegant. It looks good beside the brownish tones of wood.

CONCISE ENCYCLOPEDIA OF FURNITURE
World Mirrors

Colors

TEN HELPFUL HINTS

1 In rooms without too much light, pink—one of the warmer colors—allows us to introduce warm, dynamic contrasts.

2 Intense red is vibrant and energetic, an ideal color for living and dining rooms.

3 A red carpet is an excellent decorative element in any room. It gives warmth and color.

4 If an object is to stand out, it should be painted red.

5 Dark reds, like burgundy, are perfect for combining with golden tones to create sumptuous and elegant rooms.

6 Red is widely used in modern, cutting edge interior designs because of its energy and dynamic feel.

7 Red is a powerful eye-catcher: it must not be used in great quantities. Often, just a little dash is sufficient.

8 Natural red tones, unlike intense reds, are far more subtle and understated. They are especially appropriate for rustic homes.

9 Combining red with its complementary color, green, produces a vibrant effect suitable for rooms where there is much activity, such as the dining room.

10 Pink offers many possibilities in the world of decoration. Though less daring than red, it is warm and easy to combine.

The work study must be a room that puts comfort first. The walls will be lined with books, magazines, and papers on shelves, or neatly stored in drawers. Adequate lighting is fundamental.

Blues

Blue skies, blue seas. Nature is overflowing with vast blue spaces. Indeed, blue is the most plentiful color on earth, and its range of tones is extensive. Because of its natural connotations, blue transmits peace, tranquility, freshness, purity, and, in addition to such positive sensations, combines well with all other colors. Blue is the most neutral of the primary colors. Its association with the sea gives it depth, while sky blue connotes purity.

Blue is a suitable color for any room in the home. Curiously, when our bedroom is painted blue, it is said that we remember more of our dreams. A dining room in blue should be an airy, tranquil room. It is especially fitting for the bathroom and kitchen because it is a hygienic color and evokes water. The color does not always have to come from the paint on the walls: you can fit blue tiles or have bluish crockery.

Be careful choosing shades of blue and where to place them. Medium-range pure blues could turn out to be too pure; mixing in red, orange, yellow, violet, or green nuances should avoid this effect. A blue hue that is out of tone could make a room seem dark or cold.

Blue is very soft on the eye. It is soothing and makes us feel comfortable. Saturated shades of blue, which include a

Blue is tranquil; it relaxes people and is perfect for decorating leisure rooms like the living room, especially if it opens out onto a garden or nature.

The family of blues

touch of cobalt or deep-sea blue, are sumptuous and elegant, fine colors for a classical ambience. Indigo blue is also a winner for classic decoration. Blue should not be combined exclusively with other blue shades, however—the result is too cold. Versatile as it is, it can be combined with other colors.

Blue has always been appreciated in the history of art, all the way back to the use of lapis lazuli by the Egyptians bares witness to this. Among modern artists who have used blue with majestic results, Wassily Kandinsky stands out. He combined shades of blue to achieve amazingly intense visual expression. Pablo Picasso went through a blue period and showed us how rich paintings of only one color can be.

Blue is a classic color for bathrooms because of its association with water, its cleanliness, and the way it effortlessly combines with white. With it bathroom decorations can be elegant and timeless.

Correctly used, blue can be a warm color in kitchens and bathrooms. However, it can also be combined with white and gray tones.

Blue is a primary color.
It is the most relaxing color in the primary color spectrum.
It is used therapeutically to reduce blood pressure and inflammations.
Its complementary color is orange.
It symbolizes relaxation, tranquility, vastness, and freshness.
We can find it in nature: sky, sea, cobalt, sapphire, lapis lazuli.

DO

Use blue to make walls and objects seem farther away, or to make them less important.

In rooms where blue seems too cold, introduce a touch of warmth using yellow and orange.

DO NOT

Combine grayish blues that can be on the sad side with cold tones; they can be made more cheerful by mixing them with warm or neutral tones.

Do not combine blue with red, dark blue with orange, or grayish blue with a yellowish red. These mixtures produce a vibrating effect that can be annoying and is unsuitable for home decoration.

Do not decorate rooms without natural light in blue. Though they may seem bigger, they will be lacking in personality.

The family of blues

Sky and **pastel blues** make rooms brighter and feel more spacious. They are appropriate for small rooms. This range also includes blues with a touch of red (warmth) in their composition, making them specially suitable for dark, cold rooms. They are refreshing, subtle tones, easy to combine and adaptable to all types of rooms.

Turquoise and **aquamarine blues** have a high level of green in their composition. Logically, they combine well with greens and their derivatives, as well as with colors between orange and red, the complements of blue and green respectively. They also team up well with violet and yellow tones, creating a fresh, fun atmosphere. Turquoise is serene and adds a touch of freshness to any room. It combines well with natural materials like wood.

Lavender blue has a pinkish hue. It is one of the warm variations, very suitable for rustic or soothing spaces.

Indigo and **deep-sea blue** are intense. Their strong personality means they are ideal for dining rooms and living rooms. They can be tamed by adding white to their composition, making them easier to use and match with other colors. Intense tones must always be combined with equally intense tones (unless they are first diluted with white).

Grayish blues are highly becoming in elegant spaces.

Colors

Blue tones make rooms cozier and livelier at the same time. They aid rest and relaxation .

TEN HELPFUL HINTS

1 To make a room more harmonious, combine blue with colors of an equal intensity; for example, sky blue with pale green.

2 If we want to create fun contrasts, we can match blue with complementary tones: terracotta, yellows, or oranges.

3 Blue diffuses and softens intense daylight. It calms brightly lit rooms.

4 Blue, because of its capacity to calm, is ideal for decorating rooms that must be tranquil and enable concentration, such as offices.

5 Light, cold tones, like sky blue, make a small room seem more spacious.

6 We will use the warmer shades of blue, like the violet blues, to decorate small rooms with no natural light. Pure blue and grayish blue are tepid without natural light.

7 We may use blue in the bathroom because of its association with cleanliness and water. A touch of warmth must be added so that the room does not seem too cold.

8 Blue works well in the kitchen, either on the tiles or crockery. It teams up well with stainless steel, an increasingly common decorative material.

9 Blue mixed with white brings to mind the sea and fresh air. If we also add a touch of red, this dynamic dash of color will provide ideal decoration for a beach house, or for a room with paintings of the sea.

10 Dark blue tones, such as marine or cobalt blue, are so warm they create plush ambiences.

Together with pink, blue has been used traditionally for babies' bedrooms. It creates a pleasant, secure atmosphere.

Greens

Just going out into a garden or a forest will reveal to us the infinite range of greens nature treats us to: leaves, stems, moss, grass. Each one has its own distinct tone but they are all in harmony. Nature mixes its greens creatively, and the same is possible in home decoration. Observing a scene helps us create a balanced color composition, and, likewise, looking at a natural landscape, or a plant, will help us get the greens right in our home. Green is different from other colors in that it allows us to create an atmosphere by combining different shades of only one color.

The dominating green tone we choose for a room depends on how we are going to use it. Light and bright greens are intrinsically youthful and fresh. Dark greens, like olive or moss green, are more formal and imposing. Nature shows us that greens combine with reds and pinks, as well as with different tones (pastels and turquoise shades) of its complement, blue.

Trees and plants provide a touch of life and oxygen in the streets and squares of our towns and cities. We like to live in contact with nature, and it is fundamental that this link is carried over to our homes. Green in interior design makes the rooms more natural and gives them a breath of freshness. If a room is near the garden, or the outside, green means you flow from inside to outside. In bedrooms, it creates an elegant look.

Green, like blue, is soothing and serene. The different varieties, some of which can be defined as neutral and therefore especially useful for decoration, are always homey.

Among painters who have brought out the best in green on their canvases, Monet stands out. He showed us all the greens imaginable in a garden and how they were influenced by light. Cézanne was inspired by natural landscapes and converted green, in all its variations, into the key ingredient of many of his greatest works.

Combining green with yellow or golden shades creates elegant, classic, and timeless spaces.

The family of greens

Green is a secondary color (formed by mixing blue and yellow).
We can define it as the color of nature.
It is used in therapy to calm people and to give a sense of well-being.
Its complementary color is red.
It symbolizes peace, freshness, jealousy, innocence, harmony, and naturalness.
We can find it in nature: leaves, moss, grass, and emeralds are all green.

DO

Take advantage of green's natural quality to link together indoors and outdoors in your home.

Combine it with its complementary color, red, to create a vibrating effect and a sense of movement.

Combine it with pinks, yellows, reds, and even other shades of green, inspired by the ideas nature gives us.

DO NOT

Paint objects or walls green if we want them to be focal points. Green is a neutral tone that will push them into the background.

Combine too many shades of green in one space. Green alone can seem boring and too neutral.

Combine green with purplish or magenta tones. Though an interesting contrast is created, it can be tricky to get this color scheme right when decorating.

xey
FAGOR

HOLA

The family of greens

The lightest green tones, such as **sage** and **pistachio**, have a high white content and combine well with neutral colors like pale pink and shades of gold. Mixed with yellows, these greens provide luminosity and warmth to dark rooms.

Citrus green tones, such as **lime green**, combine well with each other. They show a great sense of vitality. They can be combined with yellows, blues or reds. Earth tones strengthen the impact of these greens.

Apple green is a warm Mediterranean variation. It combines well with intense blue or yellow, creating atmospheres reminiscent of the shore. This hue is especially suitable for rustic ambiences. It is a happy, lively color.

Strong green tones, like **emerald green** or **bottle green**, must be combined with intense, dark reds, oranges, or yellows: colors that nature mixes together so fabulously in flowers. When we use the same colors in rooms with little light, we should combine them with white to ensure the room feels bright enough.

Grayish or **brownish greens** must be used cautiously because they tend to darken cold rooms. They are, however, good for combining with natural materials of a brownish or reddish tone, like terracotta or wood. As for furniture, these tones work well with light modern-style furniture. If we want to give an informal touch to rooms where these colors dominate, we can add a dash of cream.

TEN HELPFUL HINTS

1 Nature offers us endless combinations of green that we can use as models for our decoration scheme.

2 Intense and brilliant greens give a sprightly feeling to rooms. Dark greens, on the other hand, are more restrained.

3 Green is the ideal color to link outdoors with indoors, especially in rooms looking out into a garden or over trees.

4 Green, as nature so beautifully shows us, teams up well with the colors of flowers. Following the same scheme in our home decoration will give us fresh, natural rooms.

5 Half tones and dark greens, like olive and moss green, are best for a "country" look because they combine well with browns, earth tones, and neutral shades that tend to dominate in these ambiences.

6 The most intense and luminous greens, like lime and pistachio, are reminiscent of Mediterranean coastlines. They have a soothing, summery look.

7 Green is ideal for decorating, tranquil spaces because of its association with blossoming flowers and spring.

8 Some green tones are quite neutral and can easily be paired with other colors.

9 Soft, light green tones produce unpretentious, calm ambiences, where you can feel at home.

10 Combining green with turquoise or pastel blue is ideal for creating an atmosphere in which you can concentrate, such as a library or study.

Black

Black is the color produced when an object absorbs all the light waves it receives; nothing is reflected back. It is the color par excellence for contrasts. Next to other colors, especially warm ones, it creates highly expressive combinations. It is not, however, suitable for covering vast surface areas in our home.

Black produces marked contrasts, a very useful decorative recourse.

Colors

Black combines particularly well with gray, creating elegant ambiences.

Decorating with black requires having your ideas clear at the outset. It is a color that requires experience or a special predisposition if you are to get the decoration right. It is difficult to imagine the final result, and a mistake would be difficult to rectify. To paint over black requires a few undercoats of a light color before you can even start to apply the chosen color.

However, despite this word of caution, decorating in black or in other dark colors can pay off handsomely because of the striking results when the room is done well: with a lot of daylight or well-placed artificial light and complementary architectural features.

In wide spaces black is useful because it enables us to highlight certain areas, and to give a sensation of depth. It is not recommendable for small, dim rooms like foyers, however, because we would feel hemmed in.

Black is suitable for introducing contrast and for breaking up the monotony of a room.

Black and gray tones, used in moderation in small rooms, give stimulating results.

Some shapes in a room can be highlighted by juxtaposing black against lighter colors. Carpets, curtains, and furniture in general will play a role in ensuring that the atmosphere is not too bleak or solemn.

Black on white is the perfect contrast, but contrasts with yellow and other light colors are also interesting: black is ideal for bold and striking effects.

DO

Use black to create contrasting elements in rooms that tend toward monotony.

Combine black with light colors like white, yellow, or shades of gray.

Always use black in moderation. Small quantities work well and do not make the room dim.

DO NOT

Combine black with other dark tones like brown, dark greens, or deep blue.

Use black in small rooms where there is no direct daylight (corridors and halls).

Use large amounts of black in small rooms even if they are brightly lit. Black must be used moderately.

TEN HELPFUL HINTS

1 Black is ideal for introducing a touch of contrast into a monotonous room.

2 Paint objects black when we want them to stand out or contrast with other elements.

3 Do not use black for large surface areas; it would make them too gloomy.

4 Black mixes well with gray tones to create formal, elegant atmospheres.

5 Use black in large rooms to emphasize some elements and to give a sensation of depth.

6 Do not use black in small rooms or rooms without natural light.

7 To create contrasts, use black next to light colors, such as yellow and white.

8 Black does not go well with dark hues like browns, greens, or dark blues.

9 The decision to use black must be carefully thought out. It is expensive and time-consuming to rectify afterward.

10 In small, well-lit rooms, use black with moderation.

Introduce contrasting elements in black, an unassumingly elegant color.

SPACES

foyers • rooms for relaxing

kitchens and bathrooms • color in the open air

Spaces and color

In the world of decoration it is always difficult to come up with a hard and fast set of rules because perception, closely linked to decoration, is different for everybody. Color is just as subjective: color is in the eye of the beholder. If we briefly run through the spaces and rooms in a home, and what they are used for and then check them against the properties of different colors, we will be able to find the right scheme for each space.

Foyers

All the rooms in the house designed to welcome friends and relatives should be decorated remembering that the aim is to give a positive image of ourselves. Many foyers are on the small side and receive little direct natural light so we should use light colors that make them more homey. We must never underestimate the importance of the foyer because it is the first impression we give, and we do not get a second chance to re-create it. The living room, dining room, and library—if there is one—besides carrying out their normal functions, are also used for meetings and get-togethers with friends. As these may go well into the evening or the night, artificial lighting is important. We can use darkish colors. Dark reds and greens are always tasteful, though they are associated with luxury, an image we may not wish to give. Neutral tones, such as beige or shades of white, are always enchanting and give a sense of discipline and equilibrium.

Light tones are ideal for rooms in the house that do not receive natural light, like the foyer.

31

Rooms for relaxing

Rooms designed for resting or relaxing, bedrooms and living room, need to be decorated in harmonious, peaceful tones. Blue is the best color for this purpose, but not all shades are suitable: over time, dark blues can become stressful, while light, grayish blues are too cold. We do not have to limit our choice to blues, however; many other colors are perfectly suitable for bedrooms. Pale pink, peach, beige, lavender, and violet all give a relaxing, cozy ambience. Green, like blue, is a soothing color but often it is too cold and its dark tones are not recommended. Yellow and red do not work in bedrooms; they are too stimulating.

Beige and yellow tones create a sense of ease and comfort and are ideal for rooms we relax in.

Bedrooms are ideal rooms for experimenting with color because the dominant tone is not defined exclusively by the walls. New schemes can be introduced with the bed-linen and curtains. The bed sheets and quilts do not always have to be the same color. After changing them a few times we will hit on the color that makes us feel comfortable and relaxed. This is a useful exercise for finding out which colors we like for the bed, walls, and even for our clothes.

Combining natural lighting with the right color tones can create very warm rooms.

Kitchens and bathrooms

In kitchens and bathrooms the idea of cleanliness and freshness are paramount. We must not forget, however, the aesthetics. As well as reflecting a pragmatic approach, the rooms must also feel homey.

Kitchens used to be rooms totally given over to food preparation, although today they are increasingly used as family rooms for getting together. Good lighting, backed by light colors on the walls, is suggested if we are going to cook well. Off-whites, beiges, and yellows work well.

Bathrooms often have little natural light but abundant artificial light. Like the kitchen, they also need to give a sense of serenity and cleanliness for they are a sanctuary in which we prepare ourselves before going out. Blues and whites (but not so pure that they turn out tepid), beiges, and even soft yellows are suitable for conveying this serenity. Green, though not heavily used, is satisfactory in bathrooms. You should stay away from its darker shades, however, because it makes the space seem more cramped and not so well-kept.

Combining yellow tones with natural wood colors creates elegant, cozy spaces.

The colors that evoke water, greens and blues, are ideal for bathrooms.

Natural marble teamed up with an earthy color makes a bathroom extremely welcoming.

Color in the open air

The first factor we must take into consideration when planning the decoration of an external space like a terrace or a garden is its surroundings. If we are in an urban setting, the dominant colors can be sharply contrasting: green plants, the reddish hue of brick work, the gray of nearby buildings. As terraces and gardens are mainly for relaxing, the color scheme must transmit peace and serenity—but this does not mean being downbeat or boring. Little hints of color can be introduced in flower pots, vases, garden furniture, or even a painted wood fence. The texture of the objects can also enrich the palette. Plants are a great source of color, offering a whole array of greens and the vivid colors of flower petals.

In a country setting, or on a terrace surrounded by nature, we must plan according to the dominant tones already prevailing. They are sure to be greens, browns, and

Neutral tones, like colors, ensure that garden furniture integrates into the landscape.

When thinking about the outdoor color scheme, do not forget that nature's palette is superb.

earth tones. So while in a city or town we may be quite free in our color choice, in the country we will have to remember that it is the architecture that has to adapt harmoniously to the surroundings. Natural tones give the best results, whether they are greens, browns, ochres, or any other color already naturally present. In summer and spring we can marvel at the vivid colors of the flowering plants, but we must not forget that in the fall and in winter the shades are different, less intense but equally beautiful. This means that outdoor architecture and decoration require colors for all seasons.

Having made these observations, it could seem that working on exteriors is boring, with little creativity possible. Nothing is further from the truth.

Creativity and color are fundamental for designing gardens and terraces. We must know what we want before going to a specialist who will tell us which plants will grow best in our garden (the climate must not be forgotten) and provide us with complementary tones. Modern garden designs are very respectful toward nature: they are in

Achieving harmony with natural surroundings is vital when introducing colorful elements into an outdoor setting.

favor of plants from the local area, easy to nurture, and they look natural against the setting of our garden or terrace. When you are designing your garden, open your eyes and look around; there is no better inspiration than what you see. Walking through a forest, or over the hills, will make us come up with all sorts of ideas, shapes, and colors we can incorporate into our garden or terrace, albeit on a smaller scale.

Decorating gardens and terraces also requires special care when choosing materials. Plastic furniture is quite common in gardens because it is cheap. It is difficult to integrate into a natural ambience, however. Wood and wrought iron are better bets, though they are not always the cheapest or the most hard-wearing. If you look after them well, however, they will last long enough to demonstrate their value.

When choosing paints and coverings for exteriors, try to use local, natural products, as much as possible. Using

Yellow is ideal for making an exterior as warm as the inside of our home.

Blue, a fresh, natural color, creates relaxing, harmonious outdoor spaces.

Introducing a touch of natural color, like yellow or violet, so common in flowers, adds vitality.

synthetic materials, or paints and varnishes, is often harmful to the environment, and rarely does this look better, or last longer, than traditional materials. The drawback, however, is that natural often means more expensive.

Wrought iron garden furniture looks natural and easily blends in with the landscape.

TEN HELPFUL HINTS

1 In the foyer, often a small space without natural light, light tones work well and brighten the space.

2 Since the living room and dining room receive daylight, darker tones can be used.

3 Dark greens and reds are especially suitable for an elegant atmosphere.

4 Neutral colors, off whites and beiges, are ideal for brightening up a space and making it look more disciplined.

5 Green and blue are soothing; they work well in bedrooms and living rooms.

6 Dark greens and grayish blues are not suitable for these rooms.

7 Yellow and red are energetic and stimulating. They look better in the kitchen than in the living room.

8 In the bedroom, take into consideration the color of the bedlinen; it is important in defining the space.

9 White and blue are excellent bathroom colors because of their freshness and cleanliness.

10 It is worth drawing inspiration from the colors we find around us, in flowers and plants, when decorating outdoor spaces.

Lighting

"Contemplate the dawn!
The weak light darkens the immense,
diaphanous shadows. The air tastes so delicious."

Walt Whitman

INTRODUCTION

natural light • artificial light

Introduction

When we are decorating a home or a single room, the lighting is often neglected and it is not until the end that we realize this. Good lighting is key for effective design. Well-chosen furniture, colors, textures, and patterns can all add up to nothing if we do not get the lighting right. Besides, lighting is also important for its function: it must be practical and comfortable.

The best lighting for a space is not the most surprising or theatrical effect. Insufficient lighting can cause eye-strain and physical discomfort. We must take care of our practical necessities as well as making the room look good.

Furniture shops offer a great variety of lighting systems, which satisfy every possible lighting need and enable us to do whatever we want in any particular room. Good lighting means a space can be versatile, as most interiors require a certain flexibility for different functions at different times. Different highlights, shadows, and accent lights can be used to change the mood of a room day or night. Lighting can be used to give a period setting, or a dramatic effect to a room.

The amount of light produced by a light source is measured in lux. The vast majority of products in the market state their electricity consumption in watts and light intensity (lux). Standards have been established to tell us how much light is necessary for the different areas of a house. In the kitchen 200 lux per square yards is necessary; in the living rooms, bathrooms, and hallways, the figure is 100, and approximately 50 in bedrooms. These numbers serve as a rough guide because the exact needs depend on the room's use.

We must remember that each light source produces its own kind of lighting, some more appropriate for certain activities than others. Lamps cast their light in different directions: some directly, some upward, some downward, or some indirectly, focusing it or projecting it.

Lighting must be planned with the rest of the design process. Colors, shapes, and textures are all mutually influenced by light. Surfaces reflect light in different intensities and play a direct role in how bright a space seems. As a general rule light colors—those with more white in their composition—reflect more light.

Dark colors absorb more light and require the room to be more intensely lit.

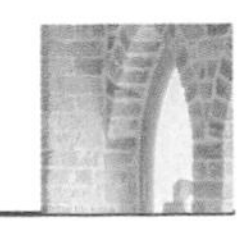

Natural light

Natural light is the first element to be considered when designing the lighting of a room. Of course, you will also have to plan artificial lighting for night.

Daylight normally comes in through windows or from balconies, though some rooms also have skylights. The angle at which light enters from determines how it illuminates objects in its path. Natural light has its own special charm because it never stays the same. Colors are brought to life by the morning sun: they are more vivid and vibrant. Afternoon light subdues the tones, which then darken as evening draws in. At night there is just a little moonlight.

Although artificial light can be effective and upbeat, daylight is indispensable if we want our home to be comfortable and relaxing. It enables us to work without stress, aware of what time of day it is and enjoying the subtle tone changes as the sun crosses the sky. It brings us closer to nature as well.

Natural light raises our spirits. Naturally lit spaces are ideal for studying or relaxing.

Windows, curtains, and blinds are key ways of controlling natural light. Their function is similar to that of lamp shades. A transparent, silk fabric can convert glaring, overpowerful, and annoying sunlight into a warming radiance that gently fills the room. A venetian blind permits us to block out the light, or to manipulate it according to our needs, darkening the room if necessary. White or light-colored fabrics or wall coverings reflect light and make a room more luminous. In contrast, if a room receives too much daylight we can use dark colors to absorb part of the excess. Moderating the light makes for a subdued atmosphere.

The quantity and type of light that enters through a window depends on which direction the window faces. Above the equator, north-facing windows receive less light year-round because they receive direct sunbeams only at the beginning of summer. East- and west-facing rooms receive frontal, horizontal light at the start of spring and fall. Light comes in at an angle as summer arrives. South-facing rooms receive more and better light. In summer, little light penetrates directly into these rooms (it is not necessary because there is so much reflected light anyway), but in winter horizontal light floods them. Southeast- and southwest-facing rooms are the best lit because in summer sunlight does not enter excessively, but in winter it reaches into every corner.

It is important we take the room's orientation into consideration when we are choosing curtains, and blinds and planning the artificial lighting. Perfect natural lighting would mean that during the day we did not have to turn on the lights at all, but unfortunately this is not always so. Artificial lighting will have to be installed, relying on sunlight as a back up. We must bear in mind that rooms in which natural light least varies during the day are the north-facing ones. Take into consideration the room's wall colors and the amount of light reflected. The placement of windows

Curtains and windows are key elements for controlling the brightness of a space. They allow us to subdue intense light or to enjoy the afternoon clarity.

is vital for achieving a unified lighting scheme. Take as an example a window situated high up and to one side of a wall. In this case the ceiling and the smaller stretch of wall will be more intensely lit while the rest of the room will be darker. A similar effect occurs when intense light enters through a window. The wall around the frame is "darkened" by the contrast because our eye cannot compensate. The solution lies in mitigating the contrast by filtering out part of the light with a curtain or a blind.

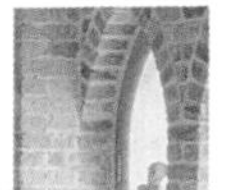

Skylights give a lot of character—as well as radiance—to a room. Normally it pushes other lighting sources into the background, eclipsing artificial lights.

Artificial light

Artificial light, quite simply, is not from the sun and can be controlled by the homeowner according to his or her needs. Most artificial lighting is electric, though fires and candles can also be used. Lighting has two principal functions: to make the home feel good and to enable us to see what we are doing. Although functionality is important, we must not forget aesthetics to make our home a comfortable place to be. Lighting enables us to modify a room and the elements within it. Good artificial lighting can give warmth to a room, a feeling of breadth, or a clear view into another part of the house (in an open-plan design). These are the possibilities that we must explore. Lighting is also key if we want to create period settings or dramatic effects. We can cast shadows onto the carvings of an antique piece of furniture, highlight the vivid colors of a tapestry or a piece of porcelain. Artificial light has the capacity to alter our perception of a space. General lighting makes a space seem bigger; specific lighting, in contrast, makes it feel smaller. Lighting can also divide an all-purpose room into smaller areas, creating separate moods.

Lighting can help us use any room for any particular pur-

Although windows with a view are important sources of lighting and decorative elements in their own right, artificial light takes over in the evening and at night. It cannot be forgotten.

Artificial lighting must fit in with the atmosphere reigning in the space.

pose. It captures that special mood for a dinner with friends, a festive celebration, or a small party at home. Soft light in the living room is ideal for starting the evening; afterward the guests go to the well-lit dining room, specially adorned with candles. To round off the night the guests come back to the living room where spotlights create centers of attention around which social groups gather. On festive occasions, the quality of light can provide sparkle and mood more than any other component of design. All these decorative tools will be possible only if the lighting has been meticulously studied and if it allows for variations to adapt to different situations.

Candles, like free-standing lamps, light up the room effectively and are highly decorative.

LIGHTING

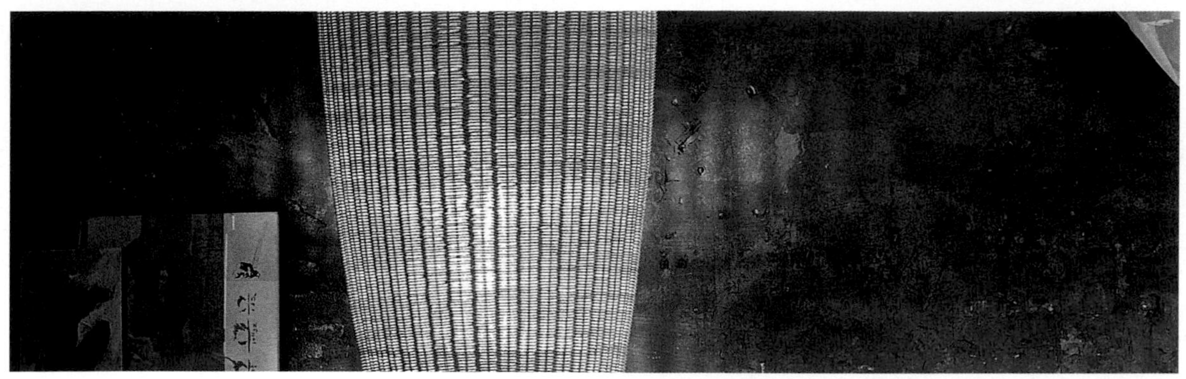

types of lighting

Planning the lighting of a room

The first basic consideration when planning a room's lighting is the capacity and state of its electrical installations. We must then consider the needs of each space, determined by the activities carried out within it. A living room is mainly a place to relax, but we must also take into account whether it is going to be used occasionally as a study, as an office, or just for reading an entertaining novel. These activities require good specific lighting. The next step is to decide where the focal points will be in the room. Some antique furniture, an eye-catching modern design, or a painting on the wall can become the central feature in a room if properly illuminated. In spaces without a single, defined purpose, or lacking in cohesion, we can use ambient lighting to unify the room.

We can buy all kinds of electric light bulbs and lamps. Each one creates its own distinct tone and lighting style. There are basically two types of lighting for modern interiors: incandescent and fluorescent. The former is somewhat redder than daylight but contains all the colors in the spectrum. When buying lighting material we must find out what type of light it produces to make sure it adapts to the total decoration scheme. Another question is finding lighting appropriate for the activities. For example, a whitish light is not suitable for reading or writing because it can create a harsh glare. A blue-toned bulb works much better. It "calms" the paper and gives off a relaxing glow.

Another important feature during the planning stage is to install versatile lighting; the rooms may require flexibility as different members of the family carry out different activities. For example, sometimes a bedroom may be a place for relaxing or sleeping every night (and this calls for soft lighting) but at other times it can be used as a study or office and will need specific lighting.

We must distinguish between three types of lighting:

Ambient lighting is in the background. Its function is to create a balanced, unified atmosphere and is normally obtained from ceiling lamps or wall-mounted lights.

Specific lighting is the light necessary to carry out a specific function like eating, preparing food, or reading. It comes from halogen spotlights, fluorescent tubes, table lamps, or free-standing lamps.

Decorative illumination has only an aesthetic role, such as directing our attention to a certain piece of furniture, a picture, or an architectural feature. Wall-mounted lighting can be fitted above paintings, and spotlights can be focused on pieces of furniture. Light sources are elements of decoration in their own right. A fine example are candles, widely used for their aesthetic contribution in addition to their functional value.

As well as providing light, lamps are decorative objects, so we must not only examine the light they produce but also ensure that they contribute to the wrong ambience.

Lamps are decorative objects. They must be compatible both in style and in the light they provide with the rest of the décor .

When we are planning the lighting in a room we should remember that nearly all lamps available have dimming controls: the light intensity can be controlled according to our needs. The more flexible the lighting is, the better it will meet our needs and make us comfortable. Flexibility in a lighting scheme also means that the lights can be turned on independently of each other or all together at the same time.

The final step is to ensure that the cables are not in the way. or unsightly. As a general rule we should place a lightswitch by the door of each room, one by the bed, or the sofa, or wherever we are going to spend a lot of time (perhaps the office or desk), and one on every wall. If the wall is very long, there can be more than one switch but this will depend on the furniture and other decorative elements. Do not fall short in light management. In rooms like the kitchen and bathroom, where appliances have to be plugged in, make sure the plugs are away from water. The best places are near countertops, especially in the kitchen, and behind the dishwasher and fridge.

Do not forget children are not as tall as adults. When installing the lamps, put them at a suitable height for all family members making sure to avoid glare. Children may knock over free-standing lamps or table lamps, so be careful where you place them.

The success of a lighting scheme depends not only on fitting the right lamps but also on placing them in the exact position and having enough switches.

Lighting is especially important in homes with stimulating architectural features or interesting furniture, because it highlights their charm.

Special architecture calls for special lighting. Light must always focus attention where it is due.

Types of lighting

The different types of lighting are designed to satisfy the needs of all the activities that may be carried out in a house.

Lamps, ceiling lights, luminaires, and spotlights are all different types of supports for the light bulb or the tube. Incandescent lamps produce light that is then projected or diffused depending on the design of the lamp shade (if there is one). Today's designers are using new lighting techniques to create new models, constantly improving the products available.

Lighting not only depends on the bulb. The lamp shade determines how light is spread. Shades that diffuse light without forming a beam or that establish a clean beam are called diffusers. Alternatively, some shades, or reflectors, project the light. Shades can be wall-mounted or free-standing.

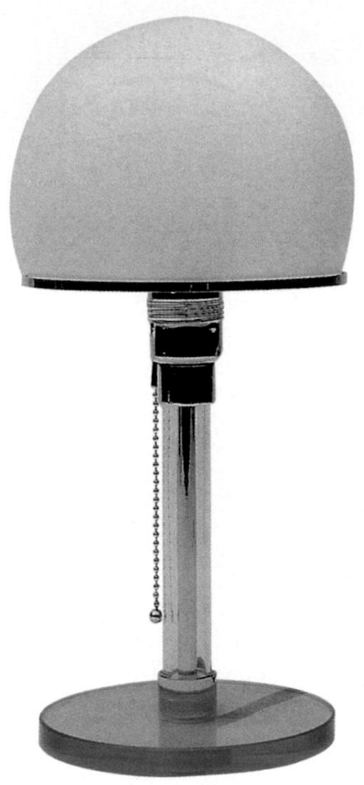

Electric light

How much light?

Electric light

There are two types of lights, which were distinguished by how the light is produced: incandescent lights and discharge lamps.

Incandescent lights produce light by running electric current through a tungsten filament, heating it up until it produces luminous energy (it glows). The classic light bulb, with its yellowish warm light, is an example of this process. There are other incandescent lamps in tube form that are not commonly used for home decoration.

Discharge lamps are based on the luminescence created when an electric charge runs through a gas. Neon tubes and fluorescent tubes are the most common forms. (They are also found in ampule shapes but these produce luminescence using mercury vapor.) Since fluorescent light has an uneven spectrum, colors tend to appear distorted—their light is whiter, bluer, and colder. Incandescent bulbs give off heat but discharge lamps do not. The fact that these differences exist should not spoil our choice. There are so many varieties, we are sure to find what we are looking for. Often a mixture of the two is the best way of achieving our needs.

HISTORIA DEL MUEBLE

Light helps us bring out the characteristics of a space. Here the fluorescent lighting emphasizes the building's industrial origins.

 How much light?

Studying the physical parameters of light helps us to understand better how it works and how we can take advantage of its qualities when decorating our house.

The intensity of the illumination is directly related to the amount of light. If a lamp produces a lot of light, or abundant light enters through the window, the illumination is intense. Dazzle occurs when too much light enters our eyes, or when the contrast between an intensely lit zone and a dark zone is too great for our eyes to adjust. It is wrong to think that adding more lamps or producing more light will improve the illumination. Over-lit rooms are too be avoided as much as dimly lit rooms; both cause physical discomfort. A good lighting scheme must have some variety in highlights, shadows, and accent lights to avoid monotony. We do not have to rely only on portable lamps: recessed lighting, lighting coves, and architectural lighting in general can also be controlled efficiently.

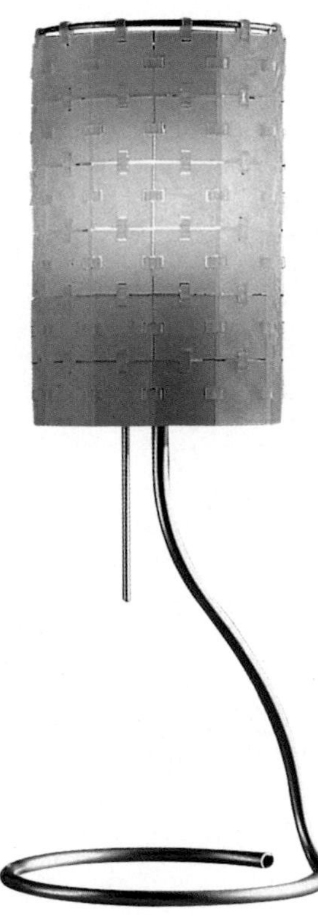

NUEVA YORK
LA REGENTA

A reflection is produced when light hits a surface and part of it bounces back. There are two types of reflection, depending on the surface:

Directed reflection occurs when light bounces off a shiny surface like a mirror or a silver plate. This glare dazzles because all the light is concentrated in one direction. It is not a useful effect for decoration purposes and we will avoid it as much as possible.

Diffused reflection occurs when light is projected onto a matte surface, like a brick wall or painting. The light that comes off the surface travels in all directions and diffuses throughout the space. The intensity of this reflection is determined by the surface color: dark colors reflect less light, which is why rooms lacking in natural light should be painted in light tones. White, the best reflector, throws back 80% to 90% of the light it receives. Dark colors can reflect around 20%.

Reflection permits us to light up a space using what we call indirect illumination. As the name suggests, it is based on taking advantage of the light thrown back from the surfaces in a room. When light from a spotlight hits a white wall it comes back and illuminates the space. Ambient lighting is thus produced by reflection. It is not sufficient, however, for specific lighting (for example, you should not use it for reading) but is useful for creating a particular atmosphere or mood.

When we illuminate a room, we have to think about the colors of the decoration, too. These colors reflect and distribute light and can help to make the room a design success.

LAMPS

table lamps • free-standing lamps • ceiling lamps

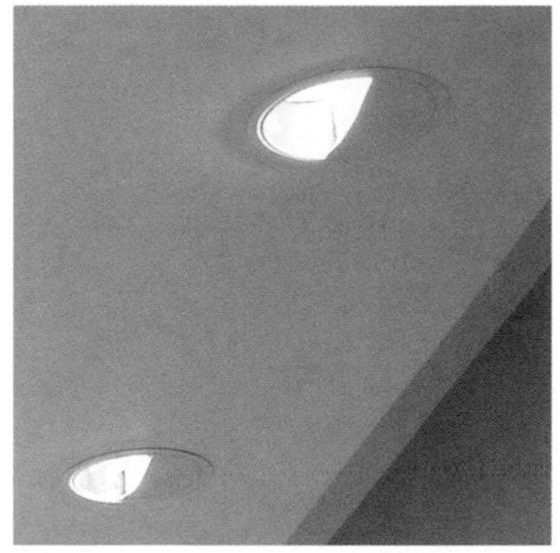
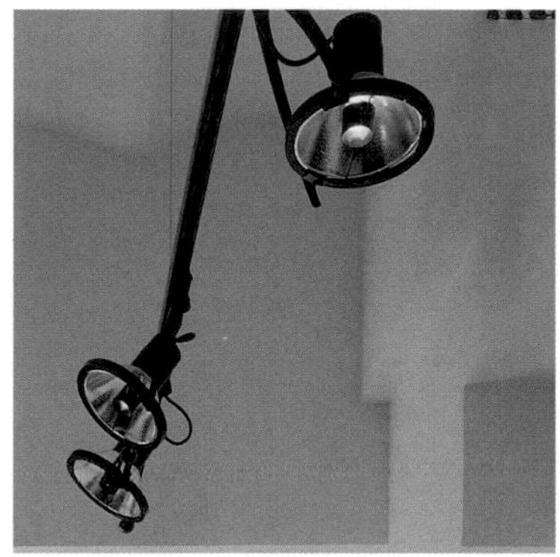

recessed lighting • tracks lighting • spotlights

• wall-mounted lamps •

Table lamps

Table lamps are light sources designed to be placed on a shelf, bookcase, table, sideboard, or any other kind of horizontal surface. They normally have a base, a pole, and a head. The functionality and aesthetics of this type of lamp are varied and depend on the strength of the lamp and its shade. They give off light over a concrete, limited area and are often used to illuminate something you wish to draw attention to. Table lamps are good tools for providing the lighting necessary for a specific task, such as reading or sewing. Be careful where you place the light source so that it does not produce annoying shadows. If the lamp is only for decorative purposes, the color of the shade will be determined solely by aesthetic criteria. Alternatively, if it is to be a functional lamp, choose a shade that filters enough light suitable for the activity being carried out. Some types of light can provoke eyestrain. Because table lamps provide specific lighting, they are ideal for complementing ambient lighting.

Lamps

Iole tavolo. Ernesto Gismondi & Giancarlo Fesina.

City. Studio Veart.

Masha tavolo. Jeannot Cerutti.

Cuma tavolo. Ugo La Pietra.

Free-standing lamps

Free-standing lamps are usually tall, thin structures like the one seen on the right. As they need no kind of outer support—they have their own base to prevent them from toppling—they are an important decorative element in their own right. Their great advantage is that they are independent, which means portable, and eclectic. They make the space where they are installed more versatile and permit the room to be used for different activities during the day.

There are so many free-standing lamps in the market it is difficult to know what type of light they produce. Some give off a light similar to that of table lamps, others project it up toward the ceiling or down onto the floor. Some free-standing lamps can create ambient lighting. Whatever we are looking for, we are virtually certain to find one that fits our needs. Both free-standing lamps and table lamps provide support. They are ideal for decorating a corner, placing next to a reading chair, or beefing up the ambient lighting of a dining room. Normally they are height-adjustable, which makes them even more practical and versatile. Some lamps include a dimmer control so you can adjust the light intensity to meet your needs.

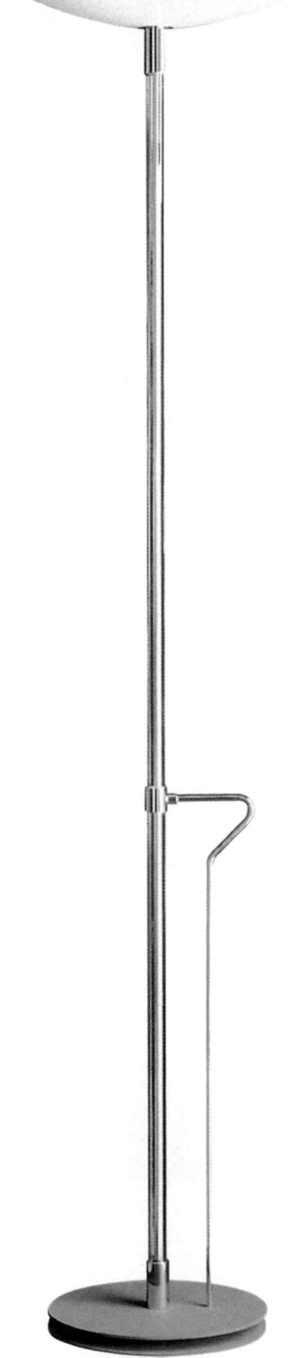

SINGER
SINGER

Ceiling lamps

Ceiling-mounted lighting, traditionally very common, creates unified general light which complements with specific lighting. In rooms with high ceilings this lack of intensity is even more noticeable. Use this type of overhead lighting to provide ambient light, but back it up with specific lighting for concrete tasks. While an even, overall lighting system using fixed ceiling elements is a good base to build from, it lacks character and interest. Lamp shades are part of ceiling lighting; they are excellent light diffusers, shield against glare, and also distribute the light around the room evenly. When positioning these type of lights, it is important to set them at the right height so that they do not shine in our eyes. Some lamps can be moved up and down.

Hanging lamps (also called pendant lighting) are ideal for dining tables. The light defines a cozy, social area. With a rather grand dining room, pendant lamps can help to mark off two zones. One zone is the table in the middle, and around it the rest of the room illuminated by wall-mounted lighting or free-standing lamps.

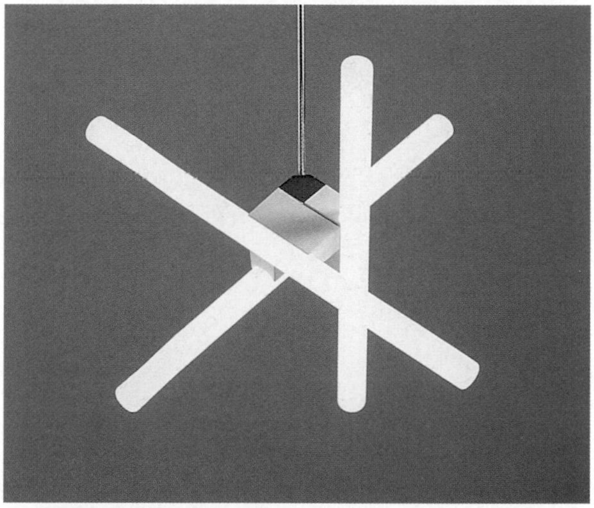

Recessed lighting

Recessed lighting is popular in interior design. It consists of a light source hidden away in the ceiling projecting its light downwards. There are many types of models on the market, some of which permit the light to be focused in a particular direction, though plain downlighters are still the most common. Some of them are not totally concealed and include a shade to diffuse the light and to avoid glare. This type of lighting is normally based on a series of spotlights distributed across the ceiling, controlled by a number of switches so that they can be turned on and off independently. Such flexibility makes the lighting effective and adaptable to our changing needs during the day.

Fixed fixtures, including recessed lights, are most commonly used for ambient lighting, and must be supplemented with portable elements, as free-standing lamps and table lamps, for specific or task, lighting.

Portable fixtures enable us to adapt the lighting to different situations. Using only spotlights, or recessed lighting, in the living room would make it a cold, austere space. Ambient lighting with task lighting is always recommended both for practical and aesthetic reasons. However, built-in recessed lighting is not totally inflexible. Many systems have dimmer controls; the mood in a room can also be managed by turning on the lights only in a certain area. Shades, bulbs, and even lenses can be changed (fitted or taken out) so that the lighting varies with our needs.

In their effort to make recessed lighting as attractive as possible, designers and architects have incorporated it into recesses, coves, cornices, and false ceilings. It then becomes purely decorative lighting aimed at making the room more interesting or dramatic, a good solution for a room that feels cold or empty.

Built-in lamps can be almost unnoticeable, but not their effects. They are ideal for spaces where we need effective yet discrete lighting, like this kitchen.

Lamps

Track Lighting

Track lighting is made up of two elements: a rail along which the light source slides, and the source itself. Logically, the defining characteristic of this type of lighting it its versatility. These systems are designed for large spaces. As they are modular, different rails can be joined together to form a long stretch, or even a square pattern.

The majority of art galleries or museum,s are illuminated by track llighting, the only system that adapts to the necessities of these spaces (remember that different exhibitions have different features). The same idea can be applied to a house. If, over time, a space for example a child's bedroom, is to undergo significant changes, or if we simply like to change the furniture and pictures often, track lighting is extremely useful.

Lamps

Spotlights

Spotlights can be set up on track lighting or used independently. In both cases, different types of light bulbs are available: normal bulbs, bulbs with a large reflector, and different-sized halogen bulbs. Smaller bulbs are the most suitable, however, because they produce a narrow beam of light ideal for illuminating objects.

Depending on how we use spotlights we can create different types of illumination and moods. If the spotlights are focused down, the shadows of the objects will be thrown onto the floor. If the shadows are bothersome, we can tilt the spotlight, elongating the shadow while cutting out the unwelcome line between penumbra and pure light. Reflections can also be avoided in this way.

Turning the light upward gives a very decorative effect. It is only good for ambient lighting, however, because rarely will the light reflected back be sufficient to carry out a specific task. This lighting system is not very practical, though, because it requires the spotlights to be placed too low. Instead, stores now sell "uplighters," free-standing lamps that shine their light off the ceiling, a type of lighting that is becoming more widespread. Of course, using the ceiling as a reflector gives it a lot of emphasis and is worth doing when the ceiling is especially interesting architecturally. Use uplighters when you want to highlight cornices or rosettes.

Spotlights aimed at the walls make rooms seem bigger. They are also decorative, especially when the walls are hung with attractive paintings, coverings, or tapestries. If we want these spotlights to illuminate wall hangings, place them near the wall. However, if you only want them to bathe the wall in soft light, place them approximately three feet away.

When spotlights are used to lighten up work areas, be sure that annoying shadows do not fall across the work surface.

Lamps

Lamps

Lighting is a key element in getting the aesthetics of a room right. In a large space, it is a good idea to install several different light sources to provide plentiful light and to create a homey mood.

Wall-mounted lamps

Wall-mounted lighting can create either ambient lighting or task lighting. Wall-mounted lighting is commonly used-to illuminate a corridor or a foyer where free-standing lamps would get in the way. It is also used to illuminate specific areas. The light produced can be focused downward, very suitable for paintings and ornaments on shelves, or upward, and is adaptable for different needs. If directed up, much of the light will be reflected off the ceiling, similar to uplighters and ceiling lighting.

TEN HELPFUL HINTS

1 Light colors reflect more light. They are especially suitable for dark rooms.

2 To make a room with overly abundant natural light less stimulating, we can use dark tones that absorb excess light.

3 Remember that artificial light sources other than electricity, such as candles and a fireplace, have an important decorative role.

4 Ambient lighting helps make a small room look bigger.

5 Specific lighting can fragment a room, which can be used to divide it into different areas for diverse functions.

6 The lighting in a room must be flexible so we can adapt it to the needs of different situations.

7 It is important to take into consideration the capacity and condition of the wiring before embarking on a lighting project.

8 Find out about the amount of light produced by a light source and its tone before choosing it

9 Each kind of activity needs a specific type of light. For example, bluish-white lighting is best for reading or studying.

10 When planning the lighting of a space do not forget the needs of children or people who need special attention or facilities.

SPACES

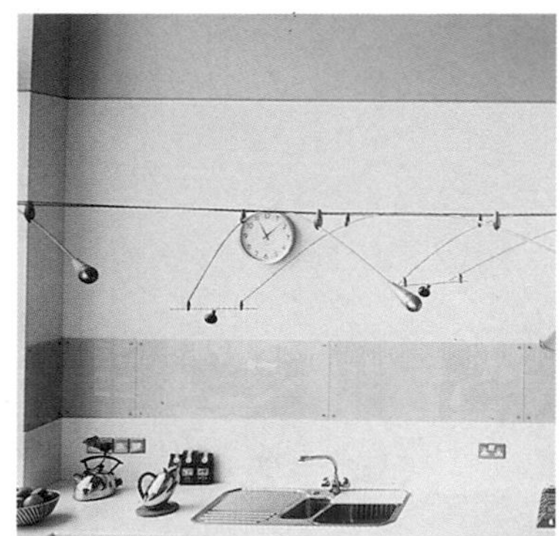

foyers and entrances • hallways and staircases • kitchens

bathrooms • dining rooms • living rooms

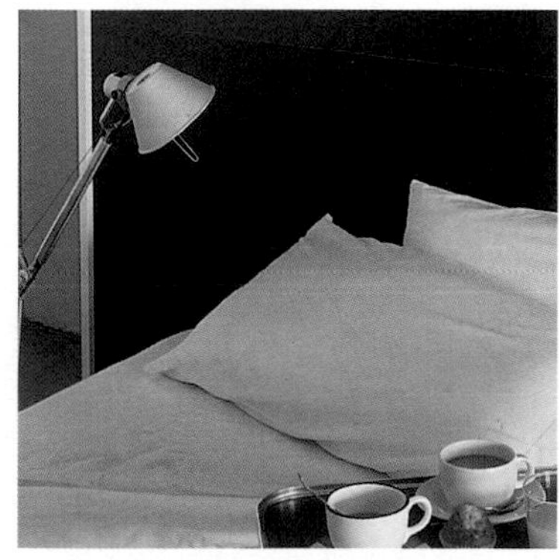

bedrooms • studies and libraries

Foyers and entrances

The entrance into a home, often neglected, is vitally important. It is the first impression that a visitor gets from our home and should produce a favorable reaction. It must reflect something about us and the way we are. We must decorate and light the entrance to be welcoming to our guests. Built-in lighting, wall-mounts, and table lamps can be combined to make everyone feel well received.

Because of its function, the foyer is the room in the house most suitable for dramatic touches, both in decoration and in lighting. Spotlights with evocative shadows or free-standing lamps that throw up curious shadows would seem out of place in other rooms. In an entrance hall, however, they fit in nicely.

Con te LE ho ScESe PErché SaPEvO

Hallways and staircases

Generally hallways are transition spaces where no specific activity is carried out and, therefore, need only adequate ambient lighting. Another thing to consider is that they are normally zones that link two different moods and lighting systems together, so they must allow the eye to adapt. Avoid sharp accents. For example, the lighting in a corridor may have to take us gently from the abundant lighting of the living room to the less intense light of an interior bathroom.

Staircases require special treatment because they are spaces in which the practical aspects of lighting outweigh the aesthetic. Often staircases do not have their own lighting and depend on the light they receive from adjacent spaces, like landings and corridors. Though we may move into a house and "inherit" this situation, we should never deliberately allow it to happen. Ambient lighting that clearly lights the steps is recommended. On the landings we can use less direct illumination, such as wall-mounted lights.

Both on staircases and in corridors, placing switches sensibly is almost as important as the lighting itself. As they are spaces we pass through, it should be simple to turn the light on and off from more than one location. To get the layout right, study the usual movements, or paths, across these spaces.

Kitchens

Kitchens are primarily work spaces that need plentiful and practical lighting. Strong overhead lighting will probably be sufficient for ambience, but it may not be enough for specific tasks. If not properly managed, overheads can provoke annoying shadows on the work counters. A light hanging over the dining table is one good solution. Countertops will need task lighting, built-in or visible. The lights must be placed either in front of, or above, the person preparing the food; otherwise they cast unwelcome shadows. Fluorescent tubes are not pretty, but they do offer effective lighting for food preparation, however, and are cheaper than spotlights. They are normally hidden below cupboards in the kitchen.

Kitchens call for practical lighting. But this does not mean we can ignore aesthetic considerations.

Bathrooms

Bathrooms are similar to kitchens. They need abundant ambient lighting, for which halogen bulbs are best because they produce a clean, bright light. The sink and mirror need good specific lighting so we can wash our face and shave comfortably. Lateral lighting works well beside a mirror, as in the dressing rooms of a theatre. We should use many low-watt bulbs rather than a few very bright bulbs, to avoid shadows.

In the bathroom we must be careful not to place plugs, switches, and light sources where water can splash them. If necessary, consult a specialist on lighting systems suitable for humid rooms.

Halogen bulbs are often used in bathrooms because they emit cold, clean blue light, ideal for this type of room.

Lighting can be part of the decoration in its own right, not just the context for it.

Dining rooms

In the dining room where food and the people who have come together to enjoy it are the first priority. The light must therefore focus attention on them. The best lighting for eating comes from above because it shows off the food, makes the glassware and cutlery sparkle, and reduces eye-strain. A lamp or chandelier, hanging over the center of the table is the best choice. If the lamp's height is adjustable, even better. But if you foresee having to move the dining table from time to time, alternative lighting arrangements must be made.

Before deciding which light to buy for a dining area, remember that visible bulbs can be unsightly. A second consideration, more relevant when installing the lamp, is its height: the light must not shine into the diners' eyes.

Light from the central lamp can be complemented with a table lamp or a free-standing lamp. Candles are another possibility. On the dining table itself, or on a nearby sideboard, they provide a burst of warmth and intimacy, very appropriate for meals with the family or close friends.

In the dining room the main lighting is general, although it can be complemented by specific lighting on special occasions.

Living rooms

The living room is the most difficult room to light because it requires effective and versatile lighting. As it is the room where so many different activities—reading, talking, eating, sewing, studying, and watching TV—are carried out, the lighting must be flexible as well as attractive. It is tricky to hit on a lighting system that adapts to each different need without any drawbacks. This could take some time and require trying out many possibilities.

Hanging ceiling lamps, previously very popular in living rooms, are now less popular. In a living room they can provoke unwelcome shadows and sometimes provide insufficient light. This problem could be overcome by adding free-standing lamps or table lights, but it is best to have good ambient lighting as the basis for a room's lighting. To get the illumination right in the living room our plan of action will be two-fold. We will ensure that ambient lighting (for just relaxing or playing) is generous. It can come from ceiling and wall-mounted spotlights or shades. This lighting can be direct, indirect, or semi-direct. The specific lighting that complements the ambient lighting will be flexible so that it can adapt to all kinds of activities: a free-standing lamp next to a chair for reading or sewing; a desk lamp for studying; a lamp atop a side table for quick, informal meals or watching TV. Think about what you do in the living room and therefore what lighting you need. Combining these two types of lighting will make the room adaptable for every type of situation. As time goes by we can fine-tune the lighting, moving it around for different situations.

Finally, we must deal with the decorative lighting, which may be part of ambient lighting or independent from it. Some examples of decorative illumination are built-in spotlights behind a cornice, lights focused on a sculpture or a picture, a wall bathed in light, or a lamp beaming its light onto the ceiling.

Bedrooms

Modern life has forced us to abandon the traditional concept of a bedroom as a place where we just sleep. Today it is a multi-functional, comfortable space symbolic of the person, or the couple, who lives there. Before all other considerations, a bedroom must be a comfortable room that allows us to relax and get back our zest for life. At the same time, today bedrooms, are often used for studying, reading, listening to music, and storing our personal possessions, particularly clothes.

First, as in most rooms in the house, it is essential to get the ambient lighting right. Be careful when fitting ceiling lamps as they may blind us when we are lying in bed. Swivel spotlights are especially useful because they allow us to focus the light where it is needed and to avoid direct vertical light over our beds.

Specific, task lighting must concentrate on the bed and on the study zone. The traditional place for bedside lighting is on nighttables, or wall-mounted lamps on either side of the bed, especially nice for reading. Be sure that the light falls on the book and that there is no uncomfortable glare. The best light source for studying is a table lamp, which can be moved around a little for flexibility.

As ambient lighting in the bedroom does not normally reach into the closets, we must design special lighting for these areas. Lamps are available that are specially designed for this purpose. Normally they have fluorescent tubes that emit a colder light, more similar to natural light.

ANDY WARHOL

Studies and libraries

Studies and libraries are principally work areas so the decorative aspects of lighting are less important than the functional elements. Aesthetics are significant in every room of the house, however, and a pragmatic approach does not have to mean poor or banal design. In rooms where we read and study, ceiling lamps do not work well because our head and arms can get in the path of the light. Free-standing and desk lamps yield the best results, especially if they have adjustable arms. They can be placed in the most comfortable position to illuminate without blinding us. Light should hit a work desk at a twenty-degree angle or greater; otherwise, it "skids" off and produces an irritating shadow. Another thing we must avoid is producing an excessive contrast between the work area and the surroundings. Contrasts can produce eye-strain.

Once we have made the light sufficiently functional, we can tackle the decorative element. Good aesthetics put us in the right mood for concentrating. Decorative lighting will hold its own in parts of the room where specific lighting is not necessary.

Natural light is ideal for studies and libraries. It can be combined with generous ambient and specific lighting for optimal results.

AALTO

A staircase and crystal shelves separate the rest area, furnished with a comfortable sofa, from the library.

OBJECTS

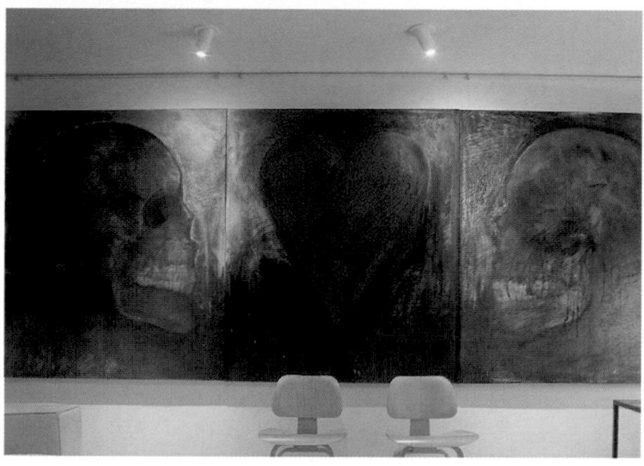

Lighting objects

Lighting's main function is practical, but it can also highlight certain objects, making them the stars of the decoration. Not all rooms will have paintings or sculptures worthy of such emphasis, but we can always shift the attention onto other decorative elements (such as a beautiful pattern on the curtains). The lighting we use for these objects will form part of the room's ambient lighting.

Lighting paintings can add a touch of distinction to many homes. There are many lamps and spotlights specially designed for illuminating pictures: the light they emit must be uniform and not reflect off the glass, varnish, or frame (it is also a question of getting the angle right so try several positions). Ceiling spotlights above paintings are a common solution, though we must take care that the frame does not cast too heavy a shadow. Spotlights mounted on track lighting are convenient because they enable us to find the best position, and also highlight a particular picture if there is more than one on the wall.

Wall-mounted lamps have the disadvantage that they tend to light up the upper-half of the picture more than the bottom-half. Specifically designed lamps that focus the light on the whole picture yield the best results. A final

Some objects, such as books, paintings, or other works of art require special, independent lighting.

option is to install wall-focused lighting in the floor. The results are dramatic, but this method is quite costly.

Lighting tapestries, contrary to what you may first think, is substantially different from illuminating paintings. This is because the light should hit the fabric at a low angle so that it produces a long shadow, which emphasizes the tapestry's texture.

Small objects, such as ornaments, vases, and other bric-a-brac, require special lighting. Little bulbs hidden away in the shelving itself are an effective solution. Adjustable-arm lamps can be mounted on the walls or on the shelves and allow us to play with the lighting placing the accent on one object or on another. Ceiling-mounted spotlights are not very suitable because a lot of the light is blocked out by the shelves.

Larger, free-standing sculptures are very important objects in the total decoration scheme. They must be carefully lit. The best policy is to try out spotlights in different positions before fixing them permanently. It is difficult to know how these objects will look once lit unless you actually see them in practice. Shadows are essential to bring out the textures of these works of art. Alternatively, if a sculpture is set against a wall, it is important to make it stand out from the background. We can consult a specialist as a last resort, or indeed just to ensure that we get the most out of our ornaments. It would be a pity to waste the potential of these pieces.

TEN HELPFUL HINTS

1 Take good care that the stair lighting is practical; the steps should be clearly visible.

2 Light switches in hallways and on staircases should be easy to find and operate.

3 In the kitchen, specific lighting is necessary above the countertops. Switches must not enter into contact with water.

4 Halogen bulbs are especially suitable for bathrooms because they produce a cold, clean light.

5 Living rooms need versatile and effective lighting, adaptable to different situations.

6 In bedrooms where we work, read, or study, we should install adequate specific lighting.

7 If we want to feature a certain object, we should light it effectively.

8 In offices, libraries, studies, and work spaces in general, decorative lighting takes a back seat to practical lighting.

9 Outside, on terraces and in gardens, the lighting must be practical and decorative, paying special attention to pathways and stairs.

10 The secret to good lighting is not in having a lot of light bulbs and lamps; rather, it lies in finding balanced lighting for each room, compatible with the room's purpose.

EXTERIORS

Lighting exteriors and gardens

We can approach the lighting of gardens and exteriors with two different objectives: to make the open air space prettier, and to enable us to enjoy it in practical ways. A well-lit exterior at night, whether it is a tidy garden or a wild forest, is extraordinarily enchanting and mysterious.

Though we could light a garden indiscriminately, without focusing special lights on certain areas, specific lighting of particular elements gives far more fascinating results. A large flower pot and an old tree are elements that take on their own magic under a beam of light at night. Or think of the intriguing dancing shadows that are thrown in so many different tones are thrown by a subtly illuminated tree or rocky wall. The beauty of effective lighting in a garden is a pleasure for our senses and the perfect backdrop for open-air summer dining. Little colored lights are common, easy to set up, and produce a fun atmosphere. Candles are the most romantic option, though not so practical, so keep them for special occasions.

You can contemplate the beauty of the garden from many points in your house. A winter's evening meal can be warmed up by decorating the garden with lanterns to create a beautiful landscape as you look out snugly from inside the comfortable house.

Besides making the garden prettier, exterior lighting can have a practical function. Pay special attention that the paths, transit zones, stairs, and other places where the ground rises and falls are well-lit. Never lose sight of the fact that what we are illuminating is the ground, not the people who walk over it. Lights focused upward would be dangerous as they blind people and prevent them from focusing properly. Lamp posts are a good solution but have the disadvantage of sometimes producing shadows.

Lights and cables in the garden are usually painted green to blend them in with the plants and trees during the day.

It is best to leave the installation to a specialist. Just because it is in the garden does not mean it is any less important or potentially less dangerous than any other electrical wiring.

If we want to light external architecture, such as a patio, avoid powerful spotlights and try to use medium light sources that blend into the building. Wall-mounted lamps or lights hanging from eaves work well. A strategically placed spotlight far off in the garden will provide an interesting contrast against a pitch-black sky and well-lit patio.

When lighting the walls of a stone building we should stay away from wall-lighting because the shadows cast take away some of the charm from the stone. The best solution is to softly light the building from afar and to cancel out the shadows with soft lighting near the wall. Take measures so as not to blind anyone in the house looking out into the garden.

Special mention has to be made of lighting for swimming pools, fountains, ponds, or anything else that contains water. Water can be lit by submerged spotlights, especially good for swimming pools. Running water, when illuminated from above, sparkles as it falls into the pond or pool below. This is just one example of the enormous decorative possibilities when lighting up a garden or an exterior. Only by experimenting will we realize what we can do and the effects we can create.

Lighting a garden is a functional as well as a decorative challenge.

TEN HELPFUL HINTS

1 External lighting has a double function: it must be practical and decorative.

2 Carefully light objects in the garden that are especially interesting and attractive.

3 Colored lights give a garden a fun, festive feeling.

4 Floating candles or lanterns beautifully illuminate and bring to life swimming pools or ponds.

5 Bear in mind we enjoy the garden not only when we are in the garden itself. It should look good from inside the house, too.

6 Pay special attention to adequately lighting the paths, stairs, and uneven ground levels in the garden or patio.

7 Spotlights must be placed so that they do not blind anyone walking in the garden.

8 When lighting facades, try to create alluring shadows that highlight the beauty of the building textures.

9 Candles can also be used in the garden, but only on special occasions and after taking precautions.

10 Swimming pools should be hit with submerged spot-lights. Also, running water lit from above sparkles as it splashes down.

SPECIAL OCCASIONS

Lighting for special occasions

We normally consider lighting as something permanent, and rarely do we pause to think about it when we are preparing a special meal or party for relatives or friends. If we stop and think for a moment, however, we will realize just how flexible and adaptable lighting can be, and how it can help us make rooms enticing and comfortable. Moreover, the lighting can create surprising aesthetic effects and capture a special mood for the occasion, something very attractive for decoration lovers.

Candles are just one of the ways you can provide special lighting for an evening. We have already encountered their warm, flickering glow, difficult for artificial light to equal in beauty. A carefully laid table decorated with candles and served with delicious food is the best gift we can offer our friends or relatives. Paper shades, very affordable, filter candle light and brighten up the room. Candles are also elegant complements for other rooms in the house, such as the bathroom where they help us relax while we soak away our stress. We can also find floating candles, beeswax candles, and incense sticks, all of which can help make our home into a soothing and pleasant place.

Candles are the ideal table complement for special occasions. As well as for their pleasant light, they are also attractive for their forms.

A chimney gives off warmth and light, producing a glowing, cozy atmosphere in a room.

Free-standing lamps, table lamps, and surface-mounted lights are normally kept in the same place, though in fact they are designed to be portable. When the style of different rooms permits it, we can experiment by moving them around.

TEN HELPFUL HINTS

1 Take advantage of light's capacity to create the right mood or ambience.

2 Candlelight is the best way of decorating a festive table.

3 In the bathroom, candles are soothing and harmonious.

4 If you have a chimney, light a fire not just for its warmth but also for the glowing light it produces.

5 A lit candle brightens up any nook or cranny.

6 For special or original lighting, try different colored light bulbs.

7 Placing a new shade on an old lamp can give it a new look. Paper shades are cheap and highly decorative.

8 To change the lighting of a room you only have to move around portable lights, such as table lamps and free-standing lamps.

9 Free-standing lamps are useful because they enable us to position a light source exactly where we need it.

10 To get good ambient lighting, combine different types of artificial and natural light.

We can experiment with lighting until we hit upon the effect we are seeking. New lamps, lanterns, and shades are just three of the options we can try